D1633872

Adopting a child in Scotland

The definitive guide to adoption

Robert Swift

Published by
British Association for Adoption & Fostering
(BAAF)
Saffron House
6–10 Kirby Street
London EC1N 8TS
www.baaf.org.uk

Charity registration 275689 (England and Wales),
SC039337 (Scotland)

British Library Cataloguing in Publication Data
A catalogue record for this book is available from
the British Library

ISBN 978 1 910039 00 7

Cover design: mecob.org
Photograph on cover posed by models by istockphoto.com
Designed by Helen Joubert Designs
Typeset by Fravashi Aga
Printed in Great Britain by T J International

BAAF is the leading UK-wide membership organisation for
all those concerned with adoption, fostering and child care
issues.

Contents

Acknowledgements

The author would like to thank Barbara Hudson and her colleagues at the BAAF Scotland office for the facts, figures and advice they have provided for this book. Thanks are due to Jim McClafferty, Katy Bradley and Jim Watters for help with legal matters, and to Ada Niddrie for putting the author in touch with contributors.

The author is grateful to Anne Black, Anne Gilchrist, Shirley Henderson, Cath Shepheard and his long-suffering wife, Fran, for their feedback on early drafts of the book.

Most of all, special thanks are due to the adoptive parents and children who have provided accounts of their own experiences and who have taken part in discussions and interviews for the purpose of this book.

About the author

Robert Swift trained as a social worker in the 1970s. He has worked in the field of adoption for many years and has served on and chaired adoption panels in local authorities and in the voluntary sector. He is currently a senior manager of social work services in a local authority and is an agency decision maker. For some years he has chaired the Association of Directors of Social Work (ADSW) sub-group on fostering and adoption and is the ADSW trustee for BAAF. He has contributed to various national policy reviews relating to adoption and fostering. Robert is an adoptive parent and a birth parent. He has previously written for BAAF under a pseudonym, and has had a number of short works of fiction published.

To the children in Scotland who are waiting
to be adopted

Foreword

**Aileen Campbell, Minister for Children and Young People,
Scottish Government**

We know that adoption can provide a permanent, loving and secure home for some of our most vulnerable children and therefore I am delighted to support this BAAF publication, providing information and personal insights about the adoption process in Scotland.

The Scottish Government's ambition is to make Scotland the best place for a child to grow up. If we are to achieve this, our children must feel loved and special in order to have a sense of trust and confidence in themselves. We know that secure attachments are necessary for a child to thrive, and children who experience a secure, loving and nurturing environment at home are far better equipped to cope with life's challenges and achieve their full potential. The Getting it Right for Every Child approach places children's wellbeing at the centre of all public services for children and should mean that every child grows up in a nurturing environment, regardless of their circumstances. Our challenge is to achieve that for the children who, for whatever reason, cannot be looked after by their birth parents.

Adoptive families across Scotland provide this love and security that children deserve and we want more children to be able to experience this. This is why we continue working with all the partners and stakeholders in the adoption sector to ensure that decisions are made more quickly and support is available for adoptive families.

Scotland's Adoption Register provides opportunities for children to be matched with families across Scotland, if they cannot be matched locally. The Register is continuing to expand its activities and runs national adoption exchange days where prospective adopters have an opportunity to learn more about children who are waiting to be adopted. The Children & Young People (Scotland) Bill proposes to place Scotland's Adoption Register on a statutory footing, and will require all adoption agencies to use the Register, in order to prevent delays in children or potential adopters being referred to it. We hope this will increase the opportunities for finding permanent homes for more children more quickly.

However, the Register in itself can only do so much and if we are going to provide secure homes for more children, we badly need to find more adopters. The Adoption and Children (Scotland) Act 2007 introduced more opportunities to adopt, particularly for single people and same sex couples, but we still need more people to come forward.

I hope that this guide to adoption in Scotland will encourage more people to consider adopting a child in Scotland, and giving them the best possible start in life.

Introduction

The purpose of this book is to provide information about how to go about adopting a child in Scotland. It can be used as a handbook for those going through the adoption process and will also be of use to those who work with adoptive parents and children in need of adoption. It gives information about who can adopt, the process of getting approved to adopt and the law relating to adoption. It also describes children who are waiting for adoptive families.

The book draws on the experiences of adoptive parents and of children who have been adopted. There are many remarkable adoptive families in Scotland; ordinary people who have learned how to be parents to children who may have had difficult life experiences. They have stories that move and inspire.

Adoption: So good we did it twice!

You tell people you have six children and they look at you aghast! There is never any need to explain that you only actually felt the pain of labour once: they are all our children; some may have blue eyes; some have brown eyes and one has grey/green eyes but hey, they're all our kids. And maybe the 23-hour labour for Calum was long, but the years of waiting for our other kids was much more painful.

We began the adoption process after discovering I could no longer have children. We had always planned on having a large family. The idea of adoption wasn't new to us: my sister is adopted; my parents fostered throughout my childhood and I have several adopted cousins. There were people who thought we should have been content because we were truly blessed with a wonderful son. It's hard to explain that need to have your life filled with children, but the important people understood, so we went ahead and enquired.

Why did we want to adopt? We wanted laughter, tears and fun to fill our days…

And eventually the process brought us our brood of three sisters. Yes, that's right, three gorgeous girls.

Life went on from there; Calum welcomed his sisters to the family with ease. He helped with the baby, played with the two older girls and actually didn't mind too much about being the only boy. Our support came from family and friends: there is no point pretending it was easy to go from one child to four in a day, because it wasn't. Life with children who have experienced the trauma our girls had endured is difficult and it doesn't stop. Amy is 16 now and still has trouble accepting the things that happened to her in her early years.

Eight years passed and we thought things were a little too quiet! The kids were getting bigger and more independent. So we started the adoption process all over again. After a while we were rewarded with two very precious children: a boy and a girl this time. That made six: two boys and four girls. Our family is complete!

It is hard; no one should ever be fooled into thinking it is easy. Adopted children are just that though, children. Our oldest daughter, Amy, told us once that she doesn't think of herself as adopted; she is ours and that's it. The problems she has have to be understood in a different context from Calum's but they are still just teenage problems. She hates us to use her adoption as an excuse for some of the things she does, and we never do; as with the rest of the children many of their difficulties come from their past, but we use this to understand their behaviour, not to condone it.

We are a family and that's all there is to it really. We have the same family problems everyone does. We could have a whole week on Jeremy Kyle with my husband asking who the father is to each of his children: but the truth is they have only one mum and dad who matter to them now, and that's us. Their past has to be part of their present but it shouldn't shape it.

Sarah, adoptive parent

Each year the Scottish Government publishes information about the number of children who are looked after. The term looked after is used in Scotland to describe children who are in care or are being supervised at home. In July 2012 over 16,000 children were looked after in Scotland. Some of these children live with their birth families and are supervised by social workers because their parents need support in caring for them. Others are cared for by relatives or friends; arrangements that are known as kinship care. Just under nine per cent are cared for in residential homes or in residential schools. Over 5,000 children were recorded as being looked after by foster carers. A small number of children are privately fostered (see Glossary). Such children are not formally looked after.

According to information held by Scottish courts, over 460 children were adopted in Scotland in 2012. In the 12 months ending 31/7/12, 272 looked after children were adopted. Other children were adopted by step-parents, a few were placed for adoption as babies with the consent of their parents and a small number were adopted from other countries.

The number of children placed for adoption is small compared to the number who are looked after. The Scottish Government and many of those working in adoption services believe that more children would benefit from being adopted. Proportionately fewer children in public care are adopted in Scotland than in other parts of the UK. Adoption can give children the love and security they need to grow into happy successful adults. Whilst many children do well in foster care and residential care, some experience lots of change and disruption during their time in public care. This can have a lasting impact on their development and can hamper their chances of reaching their potential in life.

Whilst much adoption practice in Scotland is similar to that of England, Wales and Northern Ireland, there are differences, and the legal process is very different. This book aims to give a flavour of what the experience is like in Scotland for adoptive families and for children being adopted. Almost all of the material provided by parents and children relates to adoptions in Scotland. Most of the accounts they give are very positive, but they also highlight the challenges that come with adoption.

Adoption can be rewarding and fulfilling. It is life-changing and is rarely easy. *All* families have their ups and downs, their joys, stresses and traumas, their crises, triumphs and heartbreaks. Adoptive families can have more of these than some other families. *Adopting a Child in Scotland* looks at some of the reasons for this and attempts to prepare those who wish to adopt by offering some insights about the journey that lies ahead. It also provides practical information about adoption agencies as well as sources of help and support for those affected by adoption.

1

What is adoption?

My feelings about adoption

Adoption is the best thing ever, to me. It gives children a second chance. How it's happened to me, I feel like the luckiest boy alive. I am so happy someone picked me to be part of their family. On the day I was to meet my forever mum and dad I was very excited, but scared as well, because I didn't know if we would like one another. I hid behind my older brother. Now I have been with my forever mum and dad for five years. I still don't regret going to live with them. Today I never look back and my forever parents feel like my real parents, and I love them more than anything in the world.

Sid, aged 11, adopted child

Sid's short account touches on a number of themes that are central to adoption. He mentions his *forever* family. He refers to the fear he felt at the beginning. He says he never looks back, though the fact he says this implies the past is there and is important.

Adopting a child is an enormous commitment. You become the child's parent in every sense and the child's birth parents cease in law to have any responsibility for the child. You can't hand the child back if you change your mind. Adoption is not something to be undertaken lightly; it will change your life forever. You need to think carefully about how your life will alter; the freedom you will have to give up; the cost of bringing up a child; the need to give up or cut down work, at least for a time.

The impact on the child of moving to an adoptive family is enormous, but there is also a huge impact on you as parents; you have to prepare yourself for that. Your life as you know it will soon be over! I can't do all the things I used to do, like disappearing into the conservatory to watch football! I don't get to do that so easily now. Sometimes I sit in the toilet, thinking I can skive in here with a book or a newspaper for a few minutes, but it doesn't happen because they can pick the lock and open the door. Hi Dad, peek-a-boo!

Gordon, adoptive parent of two boys

You need to think about how adoption will impact on any children you already have, on the rest of your family, and on your friends.

I have got two other birth children of my own and I think my biggest failing was that I was naive enough to think that adopting children would be the same as having birth children and that I didn't need to do a huge amount of preparation.

Dave, birth parent and adoptive parent

You need to be as sure as you can be that you will be able to see it through. Adoption is a lifelong undertaking. The small child that you can picture in your head will one day be a 12-year-old; a 17-year-old; a 35-year-old; exploring the world, getting buffeted by life and facing all those unknown challenges that lie ahead for everyone.

There are highs and lows about being a parent. Anybody thinking of adoption has to realise that life is going to turn around 360 degrees. From the day the child moves in there is no going back: your life as you know it is going to change and that is a really important point to get across. But I know we would do it all over again!

Lindsay, adoptive parent of two girls aged three and four

What is the difference between being a birth parent and an adoptive parent?

Becoming a parent is challenging for everyone. Given that there are around seven billion people in the world, you'd think the human race would have perfected the art of parenting by now – collectively we've had lots of practice! But being a mum or a dad isn't easy; some would argue that it is more difficult now than ever given the pressures that society puts on children. Children and young people are under pressure to be seen to be wearing clothes with the right labels; to belong and fit in; to try drugs and alcohol. Some are disadvantaged through poverty and lack of opportunity. There are few birth parents who do not experience periods of anxiety as they try their best to raise their children in the midst of all these pressures. There is no training to be a parent; we are all thrown in at the deep end, and it seems remarkable that the vast majority of children turn out well and find their place in the world.

Giving birth is a good start to parenthood. The period of pregnancy helps parents to prepare for what lies ahead. You know roughly when the baby will arrive; you know quite a lot about the baby; you may well know what sex it is; obviously you know it will be a newborn baby and that no-one else will have cared for it previously. You know all about its parents and extended family. When the baby is born you decide upon its name. You go through a process of bonding. In the first few scary days and weeks you get to know each other. You learn how to comfort the baby by feeding it, holding it, singing to it; you learn how the baby ticks; you *receive* your first smile; you *receive* your baby's love.

Adopting a child is different. You and the child will not have had these early experiences together. The child *might* have had positive bonding experiences with their parents, but most children in need of adoption will have experienced a turbulent, insecure start in life and many will have suffered trauma through unreliable care. Some will have been neglected or physically or sexually abused. The vast majority of children adopted in Scotland will have been in foster care after leaving their birth parents. Some may have been in foster care for one, two, three or more years. Many will have been in more than one foster care placement; they may have been in and out of care a number of times as attempts were made to support their birth parents to care for them. As a consequence of these experiences, the adopted child's love of their new parents may not come so readily as the love shown by a birth child who has been brought up in a secure happy family from the start.

It's not necessarily the life I imagined, it's not Doris Day with the picket fence and the roses around a cottage, it's not that. You start out picturing to yourself what family life will be like, but the reality is different. It has its highs and lows and joys and rewards and it becomes your life. It's maybe not what next door's is, or the person's down the street, or your sister's or your friend's. But it's unique to your family and I love the family life we have.

Lorna, adoptive parent of two boys

Foster carers provide a vital role in giving children stability and high quality care. Often even the most traumatised children learn to trust adults again and can flourish and develop positively when they are given the care they need. But when the time comes for the child to move from foster care to an adoptive family, the sense of loss and change can be difficult for the child, and indeed for the foster carers. The adoptive parents have to be prepared for this. Former foster carers can be important figures in the child's life, and it is sometimes important for the child to keep in contact with the foster carers for a time.

After our adopted son was placed with us we had periodic contact with his foster carers. Every time there was contact he would re-visit his loss associated with moving from his foster carers, because he had been with them for a long time and had had a really close bond with them. For a couple of days or more after seeing them he would talk of wanting to go back to them and say he did not want to live with us. We felt it was important to keep going with occasional contact so that he could process his feelings, rather than suppress them or pretend they weren't real. And eventually, as he bonded with us, the contact became easier. But it took a couple of years.

Evie, adoptive parent of a boy with cerebral palsy

Do birth parents have any rights after the child is adopted?

The legal rights of birth parents are extinguished by adoption, but the birth parents themselves remain *real people* for the child. Some adopted children will have memories of their birth parents. Even if children do not have actual memories of their birth parents, they will nearly always have some information about them. Those who have little or no information, including children who have been abandoned or whose parents refused to share any details with the adoption agency, might *imagine* what their parents might be like.

Now almost 18, there is a new collection of questions playing ping pong in my head. The catalyst for this was in fact medical papers which I recently read containing information about my birth, my birth mother, her family and general medical information. My parents had mentioned these papers before my Higher exams and said that I could read them once I had sat my examinations; I suppose they thought that these papers would rouse unnecessary emotions. They were right. Whilst my birth mother was pregnant with me, she did not take the usual precautions that any other expectant mother would subconsciously take such as not drinking, not smoking and not taking drugs.

Drinking	☑
Smoking	☑
Drug taking	☑

She did all of these things usually, and only reduced her intake of them when pregnant. When reading this, a wave of mixed emotions surged around me; sadness, disbelief and anger. Why would she do that? Did she really loathe me that much, to potentially damage and hurt me? I didn't know what to think.

The next point of information that sparked a fire of upset within me was when I saw written –
Doctor: I asked if she would like to see the baby, but she refused.

I suppose that it would be incredibly difficult to see, hold and touch your newborn baby and not want to love, care and cherish it immediately, so in a way I respect my birth mother for doing this. My adoptive parents had told me that she didn't want to see me. They said it would cause her too much pain and deep agony to see me, her baby. However, from my point of view, to think that your own birth mother did not want to lay eyes on you, deeply pains me. And yet again the 'Whys?'

Emily, placed for adoption at two days old

Adoptive parents cannot deny the existence of birth parents and may need to deal with some difficult questions from the child as they grow up. "Why couldn't my birth parents care for me?" "Why did they look after their other children but not me?" "Why did my mum use drugs?" "Why is my birth dad in prison?" Occasionally questions can be very difficult indeed; children may be the result of incestuous relationships, parents may have committed serious crimes, including murder, children may be disabled as a result of their parents' lifestyles before birth or because they have been subjected to abuse after birth. The adoptive parent has to be prepared for such questions.

Do adopted children have ongoing contact with their birth parents?

Whilst birth parents no longer have any rights after the child has been adopted, it is not uncommon for them to be given information abut the child's progress from time to time. This is sometimes called letterbox contact and can take the form of a letter from the adoptive parents, and sometimes photographs of the child, sent perhaps every six months or so via an adoption agency. Occasionally, it might be in the child's interests to have direct contact with birth parents, particularly if the child has a real memory of them and had a positive relationship with them, even if they were unable to bring the child up.

If it is likely that the birth parent will need this letterbox contact, or if it is felt that the child should have direct contact with the birth parent, this will be discussed with the prospective adopters. If you, as a prospective adoptive parent, feel you would not be able to manage this, then this would not be the child for you, but no adoptive parent can deny the existence, somewhere, of birth parents.

My story is unusual as I fostered John before adopting him. I am very thankful he was so young when he arrived and that I worked with his birth mother, as I have an abundance of information about his birth family that I can share with him as he grows up. I had a lovely relationship with his birth mother and due to our unique circumstances we have direct contact once a year and letterbox twice a year. This year will be our second direct contact visit, which we do at a garden centre outside our local area. Last year I was very nervous and was dreading it for all sorts of reasons. However, I needn't have worried as it went very well and hopefully this year will go just as well.

Fiona, single adoptive parent

Sometimes the child might need to have contact with other family members, perhaps a grandparent or brothers and sisters. It is not uncommon for adopted children to see siblings who may have been adopted by other families. This sense of identity can be very important for children; our relationships with our siblings are the longest we are likely to have in our lives.

How many children are waiting for adoption and where are they?

Precise figures about the number of children in Scotland waiting for adoption are not available, but it can be estimated that there are several hundred. These children have been assessed by social workers as being unable to return to the care of their birth parents, and have no suitable relatives to care for them. Children who are looked after in public care are normally the responsibility of the local authority where their birth parent lives. The local authority must have a plan for the care of the child. If the child is looked after away from home, say in foster care or in a children's home, the child is said to be looked after and accommodated. The term "looked after and accommodated" replaced the former term of being "in care" when the Children (Scotland) Act 1995 was introduced. The change in terminology was intended to reinforce the responsibilities of birth parents towards their children; the former term in care implied that parents were no longer responsible for the care of their children. The use of the term in care still persists, though not in a legal sense.

Local authorities have a duty to support parents to care for their children, wherever it is safe for them to do so, if this is in the best interests of the child. If the birth parents cannot care for the child, the local authority has to assess whether any relatives are in a position to do this. If the child cannot be safely cared for by birth parents or relatives then young children are usually placed with foster carers. A care plan should be formulated within days of the placement being made. The birth parents should be involved in drawing up the care plan, and other relevant people should also be involved. These can include relatives, health professionals, educational staff and others with particular knowledge of the child and the parents. There is a duty to assess if the child will be able to return to the care of their parents and the plan will usually set down how and when this will be achieved. The plan is reviewed regularly to see what progress is being achieved. The child's views must be taken into account if the child is able to give a view.

Why do children need care?

Children become looked after for all sorts of reasons. Parents might be experiencing a temporary crisis as a result of ill health or trauma. New parents may require lots of support to manage the task of parenthood. Mothers might be the victims of domestic abuse. Children themselves might be the victims of abuse. Even if this is the case, the local authority has a duty to try and return the child to the care of the parents if and when it is safe to do so and it is in the best interests of the child. The number of children who need care because their parents have seriously misused alcohol or drugs has increased sharply in recent years.

Sometimes parents are able to have their children back home after they have been helped with underlying issues and have shown that they are able to resume the care of the child. Sometimes this does not work out and the child has to be taken into care again. Occasionally the child may be in and out of care a number of times, for example if parents have unsettled lives and go through a succession of crises. The law states that the welfare of the child is paramount when decisions are taken about their care. It can sometimes seem to those working in this area that this core principle can get lost in the complexities of legal processes, but the law has to consider all sides and has to make judgements that can be very difficult, particularly when it seems that a parent loves the child but struggles to meet their needs.

The child's road to adoption

For children who are in care, the path to adoption is often a long and winding one. Even those children who have had relatively few care placements will have been subject to change, loss and trauma, in a way in which it can be hard for adults to appreciate. Try recalling a trauma you have experienced as an adult: the death of a loved one, the break-up of a relationship, a period of unemployment, or falling out with a close friend. Imagine how difficult it must be for a child, who may have limited or no speech, who may have been given little or no explanation of the changes they have been subjected to, who has no-one to support them and provide them with consistency during all this turbulence. It is remarkable that children in the care system turn out as well as they do!

Children given up for adoption by birth parents

Very few adopted children are relinquished by their birth parents on a voluntary basis, though this does still happen occasionally, for example if a young woman becomes pregnant unintentionally and makes an informed choice that she does not wish to bring up the child. Nowadays all parents wishing to voluntarily relinquish their child for adoption are provided with counselling and support to try and ensure that they make the decision that is right for them. Some change their mind and keep the child, perhaps when their family finds out and is more supportive than expected.

What are the children like?

Most children waiting for adoption will have some of the following characteristics:

- They will usually be over six months old. In many cases they are over two years old. Fewer people are interested in adopting older children, but some local authorities work hard to find adoptive families for older children and some children up to around 10 years old can be placed for adoption. It is uncommon for children older than 10 to be adopted, though a small number are, usually by foster carers they are already living with or by relatives or people who know them and have a relationship with them. Under Scottish law a child or young person can be adopted as long as the legal process is begun before the child's eighteenth birthday. Sometimes it is important for older children and those caring for them to formally confirm that they belong in the family. A child over the age of 12 has to give their consent to adoption. The views of children younger than this have to be taken into account.
- They will probably have been in one or more care placements.
- They may have one or more brothers and sisters and need a family who can adopt them together.

We were made aware of a sibling group of three – two young children and a much older third child and, after much heart-searching, we decided to put forward our name for consideration. We were very concerned about the age of the oldest child, but felt that the family should be kept together if possible. We were accepted and then followed joy and anxiety in equal measure!

All the way through the preparation for going to the adoption panel, we were very well supported by social work services. From approval to being linked with the children took several weeks. We had prepared a book of photographs of family and friends for the children and they had done the same for us. We met the birth parents and had photographs taken with them. Our children were much loved but had parents who were unable to care for them due to their own life problems, which meant that the children were neglected. Our children were in foster care, and it was there that we met them for the first time. We had bought little gifts for them, and as I came in through the door I heard a small voice say, "Are you going to be my new mummy?" I answered, "I think so!" We had time with the children at our home and in the foster home and also took them out. We maintained contact with the foster parents for about five years and I think that this was a good thing to do.

Jane, adoptive parent

- They will all have experienced separation, loss and trauma.
- They may have additional needs or a disability of some kind.

My name is William and I like Star Wars. I'm 13 years old. I am a happy boy with ginger hair and blue eyes. I was adopted when I was three. I am good at swimming and I have won a trophy.

I am glad I was adopted. In my adoptive family I have two brothers and a sister. I don't know where I'd be if I hadn't been adopted. Before I was adopted I lived with a foster family. I am still in contact with them.

I don't know very much about my birth family. I have six birth brothers. I see two of them now and again because they are adopted as well and we keep in touch. One day I think I'd like to find my older birth brothers. I don't know if that will be easy or difficult. I'd be a bit nervous about meeting them because I don't know how we'd get on.

I couldn't stay with my birth mum because she took drugs and alcohol. I sometimes wonder about her. I have some photos of her smiling.

I am happy with my adoptive family because I know they love me and will always care for me. I have a very funny granddad, who is always telling jokes. Some of them are a bit rude!

I have a good pal called Andy, who is my best friend. He is older than me. He takes me to the cinema and things like that. He is my buddy. I have cerebral palsy and use a wheelchair, and I need help with lots of things. I think I was born too early and that might be why I am disabled. I'm kind of cross with my birth mother sometimes. I don't understand why she kept some children and let me go.

I have to do exercises every day and sometimes I don't want to.

My brothers Jack and Tom and me like winding up our sister, Esther, but we all have lots of fun really. We know a trick to get dad giggling so he can't stop. All we have to do is look at him in a certain way.

William, aged 13, adopted young person

- Their parents may have used drugs or alcohol during pregnancy. One Scottish local authority has found that in recent years between 60 and 90 per cent of children placed with foster carers came from families where one or both parents misused drugs or alcohol. If a mother uses drugs during pregnancy the health of the unborn baby can be affected. It is not uncommon for such children to have to spend the first few weeks of their life in hospital being weaned off drugs themselves. Some children whose parents misuse drugs during pregnancy can be born prematurely and can suffer permanent damage. Babies who are born at full term can also suffer permanent brain damage as a result of their mother's misuse of drugs and alcohol. Various conditions are associated with this, including foetal alcohol syndrome, as well as more general developmental delay.
- More boys than girls are waiting for adoption; it is harder to find families for boys.
- Children who are black or from ethnic minorities are harder to place. These children tend to wait longer for adoptive families as it is the practice to try and place them with adoptive families who have a similar ethnicity, but this is not always possible. Proportionately fewer black and ethnic minority people apply to be adoptive parents.

What differences are there between adoption and fostering?

When you adopt a child you take on exactly the same rights and responsibilities as you would have for a birth child, and the child's birth parents cease to have any formal rights in relation to the child. The child acquires the right to inherit your property just as a birth child would. Children in foster care are looked after by the local authority, though the day-to-day care is entrusted to the foster carer. In certain circumstances the court can make a Permanence Order to give the foster carers the power to make certain day-to-day decisions in relation to the care of the child. If a child is subject to a Permanence Order, the birth parents still have certain rights over the child, though the court can restrict these. Many children who are cared for by foster carers, even on a long-term basis, are not subject to Permanence Orders; they may be in care on a voluntary basis with the agreement of their parents, or they might be on a Compulsory Supervision Order made by a Children's Hearing (see Chapter 6).

Children who are adopted cease to be looked after by the local authority. Ongoing support from the local authority should be provided if the adoptive parents wish this, but once an Adoption Order is made by the court the adoptive parents can make all the decisions about the child without seeking the views or permission of anyone else.

Children in long-term and permanent foster care

Some foster care placements are long-term and some are intended to be permanent. This permanence does not *guarantee* stability for the child; if a foster carer feels that they can no longer care for the child, the local authority is obliged to make other arrangements for the child's care. Before a court grants an Adoption Order it must be satisfied that adoption will safeguard the child's interests throughout their *life*, not just for their childhood. Foster care, even permanent foster care, is concerned with the care of the child for the duration of their childhood. A child ceases to be looked after when they reach the age of 18. Many children stop being looked after earlier than this. The local authority has to provide support to young people after they leave care. Many foster carers maintain contact with children they have previously fostered. Some continue caring for them either informally or through a formal agreement with the local authority.

Foster care has undergone considerable change in the last 30 years or so. Previously foster carers looked after mainly young children and received an allowance to cover the expense of caring for the child. Foster care in the modern sense grew out of less formal arrangements that had evolved for the care of children who could not stay with their own families for one reason or another. In the past, many children who could not stay with their own families, or who were presenting problematic behaviour at school or getting into trouble in the community, tended to be brought up in children's homes or in residential schools. Since the 1980s the foster care service has developed to respond to a wide range of children's needs. The number of children in residential care has fallen and the number in foster care has increased. Foster carers now receive training and some pursue qualifications. They have to meet laid down standards of care and they are supervised by social workers. They care for a range of children, including older children who may have challenging behaviour, children with disabilities, and groups of siblings. Foster carers were previously recruited and supported by local authorities in the main. In recent years there has been a growth in the number of independent agencies that recruit and support foster carers. Many of these developed in children's charities. Others are more commercial in nature, though in Scotland, by law, no fostering agency is able to make profits.

All children in foster care, whether they are placed with foster carers in local authorities or the independent sector, are looked after, in a legal sense, by a local authority. Many foster carers are called temporary foster carers and look after children while work is done with the child's birth family so that the child can go home, or sometimes until permanent arrangements for the care of the child can be made. Others are termed permanent carers and look after children on a long-term basis.

All foster carers receive an allowance, which is intended to cover the cost of looking after the child. The amount of allowance varies, but is roughly between £120 and £220 per week, depending on the age of the child. Most foster carers also receive a fee for looking after the child. This is a recompense for the time and skills of the foster carer. Again, the amount of fee varies between agencies. Foster carers cannot claim child benefit or other state benefits (except in some cases Disability Living Allowance, which is a payment for the child). Adoptive parents do not receive fostering allowances or fees, though an adoption allowance can be paid in certain circumstances.

Why are some children fostered and others adopted?

The decision about whether a child should be fostered or adopted depends on a number of factors.

All adoptions have to be approved by a court, so certain legal grounds have to be established. In brief, it must be proved that adoption will promote the child's welfare throughout his or her life. Associated with this, it must be demonstrated that the child's birth parents will be unable to meet the child's needs. The legal process of adoption often starts *after* a child has been placed with the adoptive parents.

Sometimes, even if there are grounds for adoption, a local authority may decide not to proceed with an adoption application. The court has to be satisfied that the local authority is likely to be able to find an adoptive family for the child. For some children this is not possible for a number of reasons:

- The child may not wish to be adopted.
- The child might have contact with their birth family and this might be so frequent that it makes an adoptive placement inappropriate.
- The child might be part of a sibling group. Local authorities try to keep siblings together. This is not always possible – it is difficult to find families who want to adopt large sibling groups of three or more children. Sometimes the choice is between finding separate adoptive placements or keeping the siblings together in a foster placement.
- Sometimes the child is too old for it to be realistic to find adoptive parents. The majority of adoptive applicants want to adopt young children. Even children over the age of three can sometimes be "difficult to place".
- Children sometimes remain in care so long that it becomes increasingly difficult to move them on to adoptive placements. The combination of attempts to get the child back home, the slow pace of assessment, the time it sometimes takes to write

assessment reports, the involvement of the Children's Hearing and the court process, are sometimes protracted. These delays can add up to years, by which time it may be too late to find an adoptive family for the child.

- The child may have a disability that makes it hard to find an adoptive family. Whilst some children with disabilities *are* adopted in Scotland, others have major disabilities or life-limiting conditions that make it difficult to find adoptive families for them.
- A general shortage of adoptive parents.

Is adoption or fostering better for the child?

Adoption is an emotive topic. There are those who argue that adoption is an inappropriate infringement of the rights of birth parents and should never be considered unless birth parents give their consent. Indeed, practice and legislation in much of Europe reflects this principle. In some European countries children are brought up in care settings, such as foster care, institutions and small care homes, rather than by adoptive families.

Scottish law states that the welfare of the child is paramount, even if this means going against the wishes of the parent. Many children brought up in care fare poorly in later life. As a result of the trauma they may have suffered early on, and the moves and changes they have experienced in public care, their emotional and psychological wellbeing can be affected. They are much less likely than the general population to do well in education, to find employment and to have positive, lasting relationships. They are more likely to have health problems, commit offences and spend time in prison. Modern adoption practice is based on the belief that the life chances of children are maximised when their sense of security and belonging are maximised; when we can most closely replicate a happy secure family setting for the child. If this is not possible within the birth family or the extended family, then, for some children, adoption by others can most closely match the experience the child would have if brought up by loving birth parents.

2

Who can adopt a child in Scotland?

All families are different and the law relating to who can adopt in Scotland has changed to reflect this. There are few barriers to adoption in formal legislation. The following questions from prospective adopters are fairly common.

Do I have to be married?

No! Before the Adoption and Children (Scotland) Act 2007 was introduced only single or married people could adopt, but now there are few barriers in terms of the status of prospective adopters. You can adopt if:

- You are married.
- You are a single man or woman.
- You live with someone in a settled relationship, including a same-sex relationship, and are applying to adopt together.

- You are straight or gay.
- You are disabled.

More important than your marital status, gender or sexual orientation is your ability to meet the needs of a child throughout their life. The process used by adoption agencies to assess this is described in Chapter 3.

I am a white, British male. My partner of 12 years is a white, American male. Our two children are black, adopted boys both under four years old, of dual heritage, with predominantly Afro-Caribbean parentage. Whilst our experience of being approved as an "alternative family" may not yet be typical, it does reflect a welcome softening of attitudes and the opening up of opportunities for more children to find families.

We thought that an application by a "gay couple" would be a lot more problematic than it turned out to be.

We have been well supported throughout the process. We initially found a lot of encouragement from a group called New Family Social, a UK support network for gay and lesbian adopters. Our allotted local authority social worker was wholehearted in her support and we met little resistance from other social workers, their managers and the adoption panels. We sensed some homophobic resistance at the matching stage, when the absence of a "mother" was given far greater significance than we expected. We later learned that ours was the first application from a same-sex couple heard by the panel.

Cameron, gay adoptive parent

The ability of same-sex couples to adopt children received lots of publicity when the law changed, with debates in the media about whether this was in the best interests of children. In fact, research shows that children do just as well when they are adopted by same-sex couples as when they are adopted by heterosexual couples.

Whatever your present family circumstances, the important test is whether you will be able to manage the challenges of parenting an adopted child. Some children might manage better in a single-parent household than one with two parents. If only one person is involved in making decisions about a child's life and about rules and how to handle difficult situations, this can be easier for some children. It can, of course, also be very demanding for the parent, so you need to identify the support that you will be able to draw on from family and friends and the community in which you live.

Occasionally, applicants might have unusual circumstances – for example a single applicant might live with an older parent. This is not a barrier to adoption, but of course, all these issues need to be explored as part of the assessment process.

Do I have to be a certain age?

The minimum age for anyone applying to adopt a child in Scotland is 21. There is not an upper age limit set down in legislation, although adoption agencies sometimes have an upper age limit that they set down in policy. As a rule of thumb, agencies often have a maximum difference of 45 years between the age of the child to be placed and the age of the adoptive applicants. An applicant of, say, 50 years of age could therefore be considered for a child of five or older. There are, however, no hard and fast rules about the age at which people can adopt and agencies should make a balanced decision based on a number of factors, including the health and fitness of the applicants. If the application involves two applicants, the age of both is considered, so that for example, if one applicant is older than the upper age limit of the agency the application might still be considered, depending on the health of the younger applicant.

Do I have to have a certain income or own my own home?

There are no requirements in legislation about having a certain income or owning your own home. You need to have enough space for the child to have a bedroom. You have to give details of your income and your outgoings when you are assessed; the agency needs to be satisfied that you can provide for the child. Once you adopt a child you are entitled to child benefit and family tax credits, and, if appropriate, other state benefits. In certain circumstances the local authority can pay an adoption allowance if finance is a barrier to the placement of children for adoption. This is covered in Chapter 8.

Many children who are adopted will have histories of deprivation.

The first time I moved in with my forever mum and dad was a bit nerve-wracking because I didn't know what it was going to be like and my little brother was a bit scared, but when things settled down we were really impressed with the flat and my room.

The room really blew me away, it was really cool and the main wall had a cool stencil and the walls were blue and green. The beds were separate but I asked if I could get them bunked and my forever mum and dad said yes. I was happy.

I was a bit embarrassed the first few times to say 'I love you' to my mum and dad but I got used to it and now we all say 'I love you' to one another several times a day and show affection.

The more time my mum was in the flat I grew a stronger bond with her, but when we went on holiday in October I grew a strong bond with my dad and now I look up to him

*and he sets a great example to me. I want to be like him
when I am older.*

Christopher, aged 12

What if I have health problems or am disabled?

You need to discuss this with the agency, which has to be satisfied
that you can meet the needs of the child. Remember, it is the needs
of the child that are paramount, and you do not have a *right* to
adopt. The application process includes a medical assessment and
the agency needs to take advice about particular health issues you
might have. If these are not life-limiting and are unlikely to affect
your care of the child, the agency may be reassured. The agency may
wish to talk with you about issues to do with being overweight, and
sometimes you can be asked to lose weight before considering
adoption. Sometimes, a disabled adoptive parent can provide a child
with a particular opportunity – for example, profoundly deaf
adopters adopting a profoundly deaf child.

If you have had mental health problems, the agency will talk to you
about these and check that you have the resilience to manage the
demands of an adopted child. The agency will get reports about your
medical history, including mental health. It is important to be as open
as you can be.

What if I have a criminal conviction?

Certain criminal convictions are an absolute bar to adoption. If you
have been convicted of an offence against a child or have charges
pending, you cannot adopt. If you have committed other serious
offences it is unlikely that you will be able to adopt. If you have
committed minor offences, the agency will discuss these with you to
be satisfied that you are suitable to be an adoptive parent. Some

people with criminal convictions do adopt, for example, someone who committed offences when they were younger, but has since demonstrated that they are law-abiding and lead a positive lifestyle.

What if I smoke or like a drink?

Agencies have different policies about issues relating to health and wellbeing, including the use of alcohol and cigarettes. When you apply to adopt you have to answer questions about the amount of alcohol you consume to check that this is within acceptable limits. If you smoke, or have smoked in the past, you are unlikely to be able to apply to adopt until you have given up for at least two years. This applies particularly to the adoption of babies and very young children; being brought up in a smoking environment has a serious impact on the health of children and the adoption agency has a duty to consider this.

What if we are having fertility treatment?

If you are actively pursuing fertility treatment you will be discouraged from applying to adopt. If, during the adoption process, you become pregnant, this can be just too much for you and the adopted child to cope with. Normally, adoptive applicants should have ceased fertility treatment for a period of time before adopting. You need to have learned to live with the fact of your infertility before having a child, who is not, after all, your birth child.

Sometimes, parents who have experienced the loss of a child or a still birth apply to adopt. An adopted child cannot take the place of a birth child, and the adoption agency will need to be reassured that you have worked through the grieving process as far as possible and have realistic expectations of an adopted child.

The best thing we ever did

Adoption was a life-changing experience for both of us. We were very much looking forward to having children in our lives. We could not have children of our own and did not know just what lay ahead for us in adoption. There were tears and tantrums but, for the majority of the time, there were years of joy and laughter watching as our children grew both in confidence and strength to be their own person.

The positives in adoption for us were to see that we gave a stable and loving environment for our children. To see them progress to what they are today gave us pride in their achievements. They have grown up with values, understanding and consideration for others, which they have learned from us as their parents.

Although adoption is not always easy and each child may have their own individual difficulties, at no time do we sit and consider, was this the right thing for us? It has always been, and always will be, exactly the best thing we ever did, as our children gave us an immense amount of pride in their achievements and, even now, amaze us with who they are and what they are still hoping to achieve in the future.

Cath, adoptive parent

What if I have birth children already?

Adoption agencies welcome applications from families who already have children, but you need to think carefully about the impact of adoption on all the different family members. You need to bear in mind that the adopted child will probably have had a troubled past and will, at times, be testing and demanding. You need to be sure that your birth children will be able to manage this, and that you have the emotional and physical energy to meet everyone's needs. Birth children can find the demands of the adopted child difficult – they may invade their space, take their toys, compete for attention and so on. That is not to say that these problems cannot be managed, but they can be challenging. It is important to involve any birth children in discussions about adoption and to foresee issues and carefully consider how you will deal with them. It is good to think about what sort of age difference might minimise a sense of rivalry.

Experienced parents do, of course, have the advantage of having parenting experience, and may not have a *need* to parent in the same way as other adopters might. Given that some adopted children may not give much affection back, sometimes for years, this can be a positive thing.

I think of William as my brother. He is my brother. In fact in some ways I feel closer to him than to the others now [meaning his birth brother and sister]. *I suppose it's because they have moved on. It's funny, though, because at the same time I don't think I know him so well – my relationship with him is less natural than with the others. His temper tantrums can be really annoying, but I used to lose my temper too when I was his age. I think I know how difficult it is to control yourself sometimes when you really want something and it doesn't work out.*

Robbie, birth child

Do I need to have experience of looking after children?

Assessments of adoptive parents look for evidence that applicants can meet the needs of children. You have to demonstrate that you understand the needs of children and have the potential to develop parenting skills, even if you have not been a parent before. This evidence can take the form of looking after other people's children as an aunt or uncle, or of voluntary or paid work with children.

Does it matter where I live?

People wishing to adopt a child through a Scottish adoption agency have to live in the UK. Scottish local authorities generally only consider applications from people living in Scotland, unless the applicants have some sort of connection with a particular child. Adoption law in Scotland is different from England, Wales and Northern Ireland, and cross-border adoptions are complicated, but not uncommon.

Adoptive applicants can live in urban areas or in rural areas. The assessment process looks at your involvement with the community and what support you will have. You need to think about this, whether you live in an urban area, a remote rural location or somewhere in between. If you live in a remote location, you may find that some voluntary adoption agencies cannot consider an application and you may have little choice other than to adopt through the local authority. The preparation process might be different, because it might not be possible for you to attend group training sessions.

What if I have pets?

It can be good for children to have pets and to develop a sense of responsibility by helping to care for an animal. Some adopted children benefit from the companionship of having a pet.

My adopted son is disabled and is quite socially isolated – his dog is a real and important friend.

Evie, adoptive parent

If you have pets before you adopt, the adoption agency will want to be reassured that they do not pose a risk to the child. Dogs can be territorial and can be unsettled by a newcomer to the family who is the centre of attention. The agency will want to know how you will manage this. Sometimes agencies ask for a report from a vet about the temperament of a pet. Some children might have allergies relating to pets, particularly cats, and this might affect the children you can be matched with. Some children can be cruel to animals because of their inner anger or sadness.

What if I am related to the child?

It is common for step-parents to adopt their partner's children. You do not need to go through an adoption agency to do this. You apply direct to the court. You have to give the local authority where you live notice of your intention to apply to the court for an Adoption Order. Adoptive applicants usually get a solicitor to help with the application process, but some people manage it themselves. A social worker from the local authority will come and see you, probably several times, and will compile a report for the court to consider. The process is usually straightforward compared to the adoption process for a child with whom you have no connection. But the social worker will want to discuss the reasons you have for wishing to adopt the child and make sure you have thought about the process carefully. The child's views are also taken into account and the social worker will want to talk with the child.

Most step-parent adoptions involve stepfathers wishing to adopt their female partner's children. In cases like this, the views of the birth father are considered, though, even if he objects, the application could still be granted – the welfare of the child is paramount. The social worker and the court will wish to know how the child will be able to manage the idea of having two fathers, particularly if they have contact with their birth father. The social worker will want to talk to you about alternative ways of securing the care of the child other than through adoption, to make sure that adoption is the best course of action. Adoption can offer a very positive option for the permanent care of a child, for example if the birth father is deceased or is not involved with the child's life. Adoption in circumstances like this can provide the child with a sense of security and being claimed, as well as giving him or her the right to inherit the adoptive parent's property. But adoption may not be appropriate in all cases.

The position of children who were conceived via a donor is complicated. If the mother's partner wants to adopt the child, issues can arise about whether the donor should be consulted. Specialist legal advice should be sought.

Sometimes other relatives apply to adopt. Grandparents might find that they need to take on the care of a child for one reason or another and might assume that adopting the child will give them and the child a greater sense of security and stability and safeguard the child's future. But if a grandparent adopts a child, family relations can get very complicated. Aunts and uncles become sisters and brothers and the child's birth mother or father can also become a sister or brother. It is important to think these things through, and if appropriate, to get the views of the child. Applications for adoptions by grandparents or other close relatives can be made direct to the court in the same way that step-parents can apply to adopt. A similar process is followed, including visits by a social worker to compile a report for the court.

Sometimes, if a child is looked after by the local authority, relatives or others who know the child offer to adopt or care for the child permanently. In this case, the local authority needs to assess whether the relatives can meet the needs of the child. Sometimes, these arrangements can lead to adoption, or they might lead to the child remaining looked after by the local authority, or being cared for by the relatives on a different basis.

Can I adopt a child of another race or cultural identity?

There is nothing to prevent people of one ethnicity or heritage adopting a child of another ethnicity or heritage. However, cultural identity is important and adoption agencies try to find adoptive parents who most closely match the heritage of the child. This maximises the likelihood that the child will have the support and understanding they need as they grow up in what can still be a hostile and prejudiced world. Black and minority ethnic groups are under-represented among people applying to adopt, and it is not always possible to find an adoptive family with a heritage that is similar to the child. The agency will look for an adoptive family who can celebrate and value the child's heritage and who can meet the child's needs arising from their ethnic identity.

We had no preconceived ideas or strong preferences about the age, gender or race of any children we would consider. We were prepared to trust the assessment of professionals as to what would most likely be a successful match. But it was a surprise when our elder son was proposed. We had come to accept the prevailing view about the potential harm that can be done to children who are adopted transracially. However, given the particular circumstances of our backgrounds and the multicultural network of support we enjoy, the social workers encouraged us to stay open to the possibility, as did close friends, including both parents and children of mixed race and black families.

Our decision was made easier by the certainty that our children will have many family friends who reflect a diversity of heritage, as well as many neighbourhood and school friends in the densely populated, multi-ethnic area where we live.

Cameron, white adoptive parent of two black children

Sometimes birth parents specify the religion they would like the adopted child to be brought up in. The local authority takes this into account in placing the child, but this is not the overriding consideration in matching a child with a family.

Can I adopt a child from abroad?

A small number of children from other countries are adopted by Scottish families each year. In the recent past, children have been adopted from parts of Eastern Europe, Africa, Asia, Russia and elsewhere.

The process of adopting a child from abroad is complicated. The country from which the child comes has to be satisfied that the child is going to be well cared for if they leave the country. In addition, the immigration service in the UK has to be satisfied that all is "above board". The child welfare services in Scotland have to ensure that a child, who is incredibly vulnerable because they have no ties or relationships here, will be safe. In order to adopt from abroad you must be assessed by an appropriate agency in Scotland, usually a local authority. After the assessment the local authority must formally approve you. All the written material relating to the assessment and the approval must be translated into the language of the country from which you wish to adopt. There is then a process of counter-approving your application in that country, and once this is complete there is a process of matching you with a child. This can all take a long time, so long that the assessment and checks may need to be updated more than once before you are matched with a child. The assessment process explores how you will meet the needs of a child from another country and in particular how you will preserve his or her cultural identity. It is expected, for example, that you will wish to take the child on visits to their country of origin.

Adopting a child from another country can be expensive. The local authority will usually charge a fee for the assessment – around £3,500 or sometimes rather more, and the Scottish Government also makes a charge of up to £1,675, depending on the income of applicants, for processing the application. There may also be visits to the country of the child during the matching process.

There is a public perception that there are lots of babies in need of adoption in some developing countries. However, many of these countries are developing internal fostering and adoption services and sometimes only older children or children with disabilities are available for adoption by applicants from other countries, including Scotland.

Sometimes adopters may wish to adopt relatives who live overseas. This too is complicated and the advice of an adoption agency as well as legal advice should be sought.

3

The application process

Where do I start?

Once you decide to take your interest in adoption further, you have to think about which agency to apply to. There are 32 local authorities in Scotland and they all provide a service for children in need of adoption and for people wishing to adopt, as well as for other people who may be affected by adoption, including birth parents and other relatives. In addition, there are four voluntary adoption agencies in Scotland that actively recruit adoptive families. Details of all these agencies are given in Chapter 9.

All 36 agencies have to be registered with a regulatory body called the Care Inspectorate, which visits and inspects each adoption agency periodically and publishes the inspection results. The inspections examine particular aspects of service selected from the Adoption Care Standards. All adoption agencies are expected to operate to these standards.

You can view the full standards and the inspection reports of all the adoption agencies on the Care Inspectorate website (www.scswis.com). The standards are written from the point of view of those using services. Examples relating to children include:

- You are confident that the agency goes through a proper decision-making process in choosing your new family.
- The agency involved in planning your adoption will support you after you have moved in with your new family.

Examples relating to adoptive parents include:

- You receive a quick and thorough response when you enquire about adoption.
- You are dealt with openly and sensitively if your application cannot be taken forward.

You will need to decide whether to apply to a local authority or to a voluntary adoption agency.

Applying to a local authority

If you decide to apply to a local authority this will usually be the one where you live, but some local authorities recruit adopters from outside their borders, so you may not be restricted to your own local authority. It is best to look at their websites, read their inspection reports, speak to them over the phone or ask for an information pack or a visit before making up your mind. Every local authority is required to produce an Adoption Services Plan. This sets out how it will meet the needs of children in need of adoption, children who have already been adopted, prospective adopters, parents who have already adopted children and others affected by adoption, including birth parents and relatives of adopted children.

All children who are formally looked after in public care are the responsibility of a local authority. It is the duty of the local authority to ensure that care plans are in place for these children and that if they are assessed as being in need of adoption that a family is found for them. Nearly all local authorities in Scotland have specialist social workers who recruit and support foster carers and adoptive parents. Some have combined fostering and adoption teams and others have specialist adoption and permanent care teams.

Applying to a voluntary adoption agency

The role of voluntary adoption agencies (VAAs) is primarily to recruit and support adoptive families; they do not have formal responsibility for looked after children, though they work closely with local authorities in ensuring that the needs of children who are placed with them are met. By their nature, VAAs provide specialist adoption services, though they do recruit foster carers on a limited basis as well. VAAs all have long histories of working on behalf of children and have particular identities and cultures that have evolved over the years. You need to make up your own mind about how important this is to you and you need to get a feel for the organisation for yourself, by looking at their material and speaking to their staff. Nearly all of the children placed with voluntary adoption agencies will be, or will have been, looked after by local authorities. Most of the children placed for adoption through VAAs are from Scotland, but some children from other UK countries, particularly England, are also placed with them.

VAAs charge local authorities a fee for placing a child with an adoptive family that has been approved by them. This is to cover their overhead costs, including the costs of employing social workers. (Most local authorities also charge a fee if they place a child from a different local authority with adopters they have approved.) If local authorities are able to place children with families they have recruited themselves they will tend to do this. This can mean that some children with more complex needs are placed with VAAs.

Both local authorities and VAAs can provide excellent services, and the staff who work in them are firmly committed to the needs of children. One of the key factors in determining how positive your journey through the adoption process will be is the relationship you have with the social worker who undertakes your assessment and who supports you through the process.

Taking the first step

You can make enquiries to adoption agencies by phone, email or letter. It is probably best to phone – that way you can ask questions and discuss the process, and the agency will be able to take some details about you. If there is anything that might rule you out from consideration by that agency it is best to find out at this stage. It may be, for example, that the agency is not recruiting adoptive parents for children under a certain age, and this might be important for you. The agency will normally offer to send you some information about the adoption process, the policies of the agency, and information about the children waiting for families.

Some adoption agencies hold regular open meetings to which people interested in adopting can go along and hear more about the process and find out about the children who are waiting. Often the agency will arrange for people who have already adopted to be at these meetings, and it can be very valuable to hear about their experiences when trying to decide if adoption is for you. When you call the agency they will tell you about these meetings if they have any planned. Sometimes they are in the daytime and sometimes at weekends or evenings. If the agency does not offer open meetings they may arrange to come and see you or ask you to get back in touch once you have received and considered any information they send out to you. Agencies vary in terms of how quickly they will arrange to visit you – it may be a few days or a few weeks.

The initial visit

This is sometimes called the screening visit. It is undertaken by a social worker from the adoption agency who will come and see you at your home to give you more information about adoption and what is involved, and to talk with you about the children in need of adoption. The social worker will also ask you various factual questions about your circumstances, your experience, your motivation and so on. It is a chance for you to ask questions and to help you make up your mind, not only about whether adoption is right for you, but also whether you want to apply to this particular agency. It is a good idea for you to have a list of questions to hand and to make notes of things you might want to think about or discuss later.

Neither my husband nor I had any idea of what would happen after we made enquiries with our local authority concerning adoption. We thought that we might be too old, but were pleased to be told that we were not! I picked up the phone one day in December and a few days later the two Lindas (social workers from the adoption agency) arrived! They explained the process that would lie ahead, which did not worry us...

Jane, adoptive parent

If you decide, for whatever reason, that you do not want to adopt with this agency, you can apply to another. But bear in mind that your choice of agencies will be limited – the voluntary adoption agencies do not cover the whole of Scotland, and most local authorities recruit only within their own boundaries or within easy reach of them.

The prospect of the first visit from a social worker can be a bit daunting – none of us likes to be judged and there will be an

element of that. Houses never look so clean and tidy as just before
that initial visit!

---

*Lesley (the social worker) arrived at our house to get started:
we were terrified. What if she didn't like us? You hear so
many negative things about social workers don't you? But not
Lesley. She was so laid back and immediately put us at ease.*

Sarah, adoptive parent

Occasionally the social worker might suggest that adoption is not
right for you at this time. But remember that the social worker is
keen to find adoptive families for children and will not be trying to
trip you up. Try to be relaxed and be yourself; adoption works when
real children are most closely matched with real families – there is no
point in trying to be something or someone you are not. The social
worker might also talk about fostering or other forms of care, so that
you are aware of the different ways in which you can look after
children that you might not have thought of before.

After the first visit you will normally be asked to think things over for
a while and get back to the agency if you want to proceed.
Sometimes a phone call is enough, but some agencies might ask you
to fill in an initial application form at this stage.

What checks and references will the agency carry out?

Once you have confirmed that you want to apply you will be asked
to give your written consent to enable various checks to be carried
out. These include checks with a government organisation called
Disclosure Scotland to see if you have any criminal convictions as well
as to see if the local authority holds any relevant information about
you, including whether you have received any social work services
yourself. You will also be asked to provide the details of two or more

referees who can provide information about you, particularly in relation to your experience of caring for children and the skills you have in this. The referees you choose will not normally be related to you; they should be friends or people who know you well, rather than people with whom you have a professional relationship. A reference may also be taken up from your employer if you have one. The agency will probably want to interview your referees by visiting them or speaking to them over the phone. This is all about building up a picture of you and your life and is used to assess how you would parent a child. The agency will discuss the references with you. Occasionally referees do not give permission for their views and information to be shared, particularly if it is negative. In this case the agency will be constrained in what it can tell you and this can be frustrating for applicants, particularly if it means that the agency decides it cannot take your application further, but this is rare. Sometimes, close relatives who are not living in the household might also be interviewed.

The process of approving our son and his partner as prospective adoptive parents was a positive one for us grandparents. The opportunity to affirm the qualities of our son, his partner and their relationship, as well as of the strong and varied network of support they enjoy from friends, was a pleasure. Meeting the social worker helped us to think through our own commitment to supporting their decision to adopt. This and the subsequent court hearing helped us to feel a closer connection to this evolving family and to their delightful friends and supporters.

Malcolm, father of an adoptive parent

Previous partners

If you have had previous partners and if you have children through other relationships the agency will want to understand your story. They will need to be reassured that you have handled these relationships as well as can be expected, and that there has not been any domestic violence or poor parenting in the past. The agency may wish to meet previous partners or children who no longer live with you. They will be sensitive to acrimonious break-ups of previous relationships but it is important that you discuss these events openly.

It may take some weeks to complete all of these checks. Some agencies wait until at least some of them have been completed before taking an application further. Others might offer you a training or preparation group before all the checks are returned.

Health checks

At some point in your assessment you will be required to undertake a full medical examination by your general practitioner and they will complete a report for the agency. This will outline any relevant information from your medical history, including your mental health, as well as wellbeing issues such as smoking and drinking.

If there are other adults living in the house, including any children over the age of 16, or your parents, checks, including health checks, will also need to be made into their background.

The adoption preparation group

Most adoption agencies run preparation groups for prospective adopters. The main purpose of these is to give you as much information as possible about what it will be like to adopt a child, in order to help you decide whether this is something you really want to do. Sometimes the groups will meet over a period of weeks in the evenings or at weekends. Typically, around half a dozen couples and single people attend each group. There may be warm-up exercises to help you relax and get to know one another. The group will follow a programme, which will usually explore the following themes:

- Why are we here?
- Who are the children and why do they need permanence?
- How do children learn to feel secure?
- Overcoming the effects of neglect and abuse.
- Loving, losing and keeping family links alive.
- What happens next?

Sessions may include large or small group discussions, DVDs, input from guest speakers / facilitators, case studies, "quick thinks", quizzes, etc. During the sessions there will be lots of opportunities to ask questions and there will probably be homework for you to do between sessions and articles for you to read in preparation for future sessions. If group members identify issues they want to find out more about, the group leaders should address these. The groups are usually led by two social workers from the agency, and seasoned adopters also often attend to talk about their experiences and to answer questions.

At the end of the programme the group leaders will probably provide a brief report about how you came across to them. They will note any particular skills or attitudes that it would be useful to explore during the assessment.

Nearly everyone who takes part in adoption preparation groups finds them stimulating and thought provoking, and says it helps them to think about themselves in a new way.

We went along to a preparation group, which covered what adoption meant and helped us understand the backgrounds of children looking for families and the needs that they may have. Issues, such as contact with birth parents, were

*discussed. Case studies were presented and a very real picture
was painted of what could lie ahead. The training was very
good and the people in the group were superb.*

*At the same time as this was happening, we were receiving
regular visits from our social workers. Sometimes we were
interviewed together and latterly we were interviewed
separately. We also had to provide referees who were also
visited at home and interviewed. We had medical
examinations. You need to have stamina for this! We still
need our stamina today!*

Jane, adoptive parent

If during or at the end of the preparation group process you feel
adoption is not for you, or that the time is not right, you need to feel
able to say this to the agency. They should respect your decision and
give you any support you might need to move on.

Sometimes the preparation group process can throw up issues for
those attending – participants can, for example, be surprised and
shocked when they learn about the extent of abuse that some
children experience. It is important that you talk these issues through
with the group leaders. Occasionally sessions can trigger memories
of personal experiences of trauma and loss for those attending.
Again, the agency should support you through this. The programme
for the group sessions will be given to you in advance or at the first
session, so that nothing should come as a surprise.

Not all adoption agencies run preparation groups – sometimes this
is not viable, for example in rural settings. In this case the agency
should have other ways of ensuring that you are able to work
through the preparation materials.

The assessment

The assessment is the process that explores whether adoption is right for you and your family. It should not be something that is done *to* you, but something that is done *with* you. The work you do with your social worker in the course of the assessment is summarised in a comprehensive assessment report. The assessment is a journey of exploration and you need to be open and honest with yourself and with the agency. You need to be at the heart of the process and you need to approach it as an opportunity to think honestly about your life and whether you and your family have the space, time, energy and personal and emotional capacity for adoption. Inevitably there is an element of judgement within the assessment, but the aim of the process is to reach a written summary that both you, as the applicant, and the agency can agree is accurate. The written summary of the assessment tries to evaluate what you would be like as an adoptive parent; what your strengths are; what your vulnerabilities might be; what sort of child you would be best placed to care for. It addresses a number of themes:

- Do you meet the standards of the agency to be approved as adoptive parents?
- What sort of child would you be able to care for?
- How many children would you be in a position to adopt?

Most adoption assessments (and fostering assessments) in Scotland are written using a framework or template designed by the British Association for Adoption and Fostering (BAAF), commonly known as the Form F, but some adoption agencies use different forms. The assessment report will go to the agency's adoption panel for consideration (see Chapter 4).

As well as being used to consider whether you should be approved by the agency, the Form F, or written assessment, will also be used to "match" you with a child (or children) after you have been approved. It will be read by social workers who are looking for families for children, and the content will help them decide whether you have the potential to care for these children, so it is important that you are confident that it is accurate. It will also be considered at adoption panels that look at possible matches for children. So it will be seen by quite a number of people after it has been written.

The written assessment report has a number of different sections including:

- Factual information about your names, dates of birth, addresses, occupations, incomes, etc.
- A pen picture of you and your family. Most applicants are asked to write this themselves.
- A history of each applicant. Any significant events will be discussed in this, including previous partners, other children you might have, etc.
- Your motivation to adopt including a discussion about any issues arising from infertility and treatment, and how you have managed this if this is relevant.
- Your birth children if you have any, and the possible impact of adoption on them.
- The type of children you feel able to care for. This sometimes includes a list of characteristics that children have, including whether you feel able to care for a child with disabilities, one who may have been sexually abused, one whose birth family is likely to have ongoing contact, etc.
- The social worker's summary of their assessment of you and the type of child you could care for.
- A summary of the content of the references, and information from other sources, including details of any criminal convictions.
- The medical information provided by your GP will be in a separate report, and there will be a comment from the agency's medical advisor about this.

Nothing in the assessment report should come as a surprise to you. The content should be agreed as the assessment goes along. The assessment report – the actual bit of paper – is important, but the process of exploring whether adoption is right for you is more so. If, during the assessment process, you decide that you do not want to proceed it is fine to say that – it does not imply that you are "deficient" in any way. For your own sake, and the sake of children, you need to be honest and open so that you do not get drawn into a commitment that you might regret.

Once the draft of the report is nearing completion the social worker will come to see you with a manager or senior member of staff from the agency. This manager will have looked at the draft and will talk with you about any areas that seem significant. You and the agency will each sign the report as being accurate. Some agencies attach photographs of you to the application. Some applicants prepare storybooks about themselves to supplement the content of the assessment and to bring to life what it is like to be part of their family. These can include photographs and descriptions of day-to-day family life, etc.

What if you don't agree with the assessment?

A positive assessment process will be one in which the applicants have been able to express themselves openly and honestly and they and the social worker have reached an agreed picture of what it is like to be part of their family. It will describe their strengths as potential adoptive parents, their vulnerabilities and what type of child they will be best placed to care for. Occasionally there might be areas you disagree about, perhaps to do with how the social worker views some traumatic event you might have experienced in the past, or the timing of adoption, if, for example, you have experienced some recent family upheaval. It is important to talk such issues through and reach a way of dealing with them in the report.

It is hard to be judged by others. If there are things in the report that you feel are not accurate, think about them carefully, talk with your partner, if you have one, or a friend, and talk again to the social worker. It is nearly always possible to reach a shared understanding that everyone is comfortable with.

Sometimes the social worker might recommend that you should not be approved as adoptive parents at this time. This should not come as a surprise at the end of the assessment; if the social worker believes there are issues that mean you should not adopt, they should be open with you about these at the time. You may be advised to put the assessment on hold for a while, or you may be told that you should re-apply at some point in the future; it depends on the issue. You can insist on completing the assessment, but the approval process that follows the assessment will be complicated if you and the social worker are not in agreement. Sometimes the disagreements can be resolved when the manager from the agency comes to see you, but sometimes this will reinforce the concerns that the agency has. You can present your views to the agency's adoption panel if you choose. The agency will then need to make a decision about how your application should be dealt with. Such conflicts are rare and the assessment process is usually a positive experience for applicants.

The approval process

Once the assessment has been completed it is considered by the agency's adoption panel. All local authority adoption agencies and voluntary adoption agencies (VAAs) are required to appoint an adoption panel.

In local authorities the role of the adoption panel is:

- To consider the needs of children who may be in need of adoption and to recommend whether arrangements should be made for adoption as well as how this will be secured legally.
- To recommend the matching of children with prospective adoptive parents.
- To recommend the approval of prospective adoptive parents and to specify the numbers, ages and type of children they can adopt.
- To recommend whether an adoption allowance should be payable in relation to particular children and adoption placements.

In addition to these formal responsibilities, some local authorities ask their adoption panels to look at other matters. These can include: consideration of children who may need other forms of long-term care; reviews of adoptive parents who have been approved by the agency but who have not yet had a child placed with them; and approval of foster carers who are offering long-term fostering placements for children.

VAA adoption panels have a similar responsibility to recommend the approval of adoptive parents and to specify the number and ages of children they can care for. They do not register children for adoption or formally match them with children. Both of these responsibilities rest with the local authority.

Who sits on adoption panels?

Adoption panels must contain at least six members. At least three members have to be present at each meeting for it to be quorate, i.e. for it to be able to make a recommendation. One of the members of the panel has to be appointed by the agency to act as a chairperson. The panel is required to have a medical advisor and a legal advisor.

The role of the medical advisor is:

● In relation to local authority adoption panels, to provide a comprehensive assessment of the health of children being considered for adoption. This is done in conjunction with the child's general practitioner and any specialist health professionals who are involved with the child. The medical advisor also reviews the health histories of the child's parents and known extended family, and advises about the implications of this – there might, for example, be hereditary conditions that could affect the child in the future. The medical advisor provides a summary report for the adoption panel about these issues and this is also shared with potential adoptive parents during the matching process. Comprehensive medical information about the child's birth family is not always available – sometimes the identity of the father may not be known, or the birth parents refuse to provide information. The medical advisor will highlight any such issues in their report. If there are known genetic conditions the medical advisor will provide information about these. If the child's development may have been affected by the lifestyle of the birth parents, the medical advisor will also provide information about this – for example, if the child's mother used drugs or alcohol during pregnancy. It is often not possible to predict the impact of hereditary conditions or other factors on the child's long-term development, but the medical advisor will give as much information as is possible.

- In relation to both local authorities and VAAs, the medical advisor reviews medical information about adoptive applicants and advises the adoption panel if there may be medical reasons why the applicants might not be suitable to adopt. All adoptive applicants must undertake a medical examination by their general practitioner, who will also comment on medical history, including any history of mental health and issues related to wellbeing such as smoking and use of alcohol and drugs. The medical advisor reviews all this information and advises the panel.

The medical advisor has to be a qualified medical practitioner and is usually a general practitioner or a community paediatrician. Some adoption panels have different medical advisors for children and for adoptive applicants. The medical advisor does not have to be present at the panel, but their report must be available. They are usually present when decisions are being taken about whether children should be placed for adoption, and when the panel is deciding whether a child should be matched with particular adoptive parents. They are sometimes present when the approval of adoptive applicants is under consideration.

Legal issues will be dealt with in Chapter 6, but in summary the role of the adoption panel's legal advisor is:

- In relation to local authority adoption panels, to advise the panel whether there are likely to be legal grounds for a court to agree

to the adoption of a child if the child's parents are not consenting
to the adoption.

● To advise the panel of the different legal options for securing the
child for adoption.

● In relation to adoptive applicants, to advise both local authority
and VAA panels whether there might be any legal barriers to the
approval of potential adoptive applicants – for example, in
relation to known criminal convictions, or whether the applicants
may be unable to satisfy the regulations.

As with the medical advisor, the legal advisor does not need to be
present when the panel is considering the needs of children or
looking at adoption applications. In practice the legal advisor is
usually present when the needs of children are being considered by
the adoption panel, or when the child is being matched with
adopters. It is less usual for the legal advisor to be present when the
approval of adoptive applicants is being considered.

Apart from the legal advisor and the medical advisor, the adoption
agency also has to appoint a chairperson. This is usually someone
with a background of managing fostering and adoption services or
someone with considerable experience of adoption.

Statutory guidance suggests that adoption panels should include
people with experience of the adoption system, such as experienced
adoptive parents, or people who were adopted themselves. The
panel may also include social workers who work for the agency or
sometimes for other adoption agencies. There might also be
psychologists, nursing staff, teachers, residential child care staff and
others with relevant experience and knowledge. Some local
authorities have elected councillors on their panels.

---

*I have been a member of the fostering and adoption panel for
three years. Panel members have to have a good
understanding of the importance of permanency planning
and of a child's need to feel secure and be claimed by a
prospective family.*

Placing children for adoption is a complex process and the role of a panel member is very important. Being involved in discussions which focus on the needs of the child and knowing that you are part of a decision-making process which focuses on stability and security throughout the child's lifetime is an area of work that I feel privileged to be part of.

I have the utmost respect for adoptive applicants as they share their life stories and give account of the challenges they have faced on their journey to become adoptive parents. It is extremely satisfying to see the relief on their faces when they are approved and to see how happy they are when a decision is made to place a child.

It is good to see everyone working hard to meet the needs of children. I am always reassured by the honest and upfront approach that is taken with adoptive parents and the advice and encouragement that is offered to utilise all support available.

Daphne, adoption panel member

The agency has to have a process in place to select and appoint panel members. This process will include the undertaking of checks, including criminal records checks. The membership of the panel has to be reviewed periodically and the appointment of individual members should also be subject to review and appraisal.

What is it like for adoptive applicants attending panels?

Eventually the forms were completed and signed and we waited for the adoption panel. In a few weeks we found ourselves in a room with about half a dozen panel members, along with our social worker and the agency's medical advisor. It was a bit like an interview, but everyone was very friendly and tried to put us at ease. No matter how open the process tries to be, people will talk about you in private, and it is inevitable to wonder what they really think of you. However, the process was relatively painless, even enjoyable in a funny way, and we were recommended for approval. We received our letter from the agency decision maker a few days later and it was all systems go!

Robert, adoptive parent

Adoption agencies in Scotland expect adoption applicants to be present for at least part of the panel meeting.

Panels usually meet in a council building in the case of local authorities, or in the offices of the voluntary adoption agency. You will normally meet up with your social worker before the panel and may have to wait till the panel is ready to deal with your application. Panels usually deal with a number of applications and other business when they meet. Your social worker may be asked to meet with the panel before you join them. This may be to help the panel members draw up an agenda of issues they want to discuss with you.

When you join the panel the chairperson should introduce you to those present. Some panels have systems of name cards so you can remember who's who. Some agencies will have sent you a leaflet beforehand explaining the panel process and letting you know who will be there. There will be at least three panel members, including the chairperson. Whilst the minimum number of panel members who must be present is three, most panels will have more than three members present, partly in case one panel member is unable to come at the last moment and partly to share the responsibility of the decision-making process more widely. There will be a minute taker present to make a record of the meeting. Occasionally there might be an observer, for example from the Care Inspectorate, or a student or someone in the process of being trained about adoption work. So there could be around eight or more people in the room as well as yourselves. This can feel like a nerve-wracking prospect, but the panel members are experienced people who should try to put you at ease. They, and the agency as a whole, are keen to recruit adoptive parents and they will not be trying to catch you out!

We found the panel very friendly and not intimidating at all. Of course there are a lot of faces there but they are looking towards the children's best interests; that's what you've got to remember.

Dave, adoptive parent

The panel will have all the information relevant to your application, including the written assessment (usually in the Form F). Panel members will have been sent this some days before the panel, so will have read it carefully beforehand.

The panel has to consider your application to adopt and recommend whether you should be approved, and if so for how many children and for what age range. The panel has three options:

- To recommend approval of your application.
- To defer a decision for more information or work to be done.
- To recommend that you should not be approved.

Applications are usually approved in line with the social worker's assessment and recommendation – this assessment will have been a rigorous process and will have drawn together evidence of your ability to meet the needs of an adopted child.

The role of the panel is to *scrutinise* this assessment. Panel members are detached and objective. The panel has an important role in checking that everything has been covered in the assessment and that the conclusions of the assessment are sound. It is not the role of the panel to assess you all over again, but to ensure that the assessment is well-founded. Panel members will put questions to the social worker and will wish to open up discussion about your application. They may start off by asking you why you want to adopt, how you have found the assessment process, how useful you found the preparation groups, etc. This interaction helps the panel members to get to know you; they have a big responsibility – they need to be confident that they can recommend that the agency should entrust a vulnerable child to your care for life! It is important to be yourself, to be comfortable with your assessment and to engage with the process. You will be given an opportunity to ask questions. If there is anything you do not understand you should speak up and ask. The vast majority of adoptive applicants find the panel experience positive; it is, after all, a process that confirms you have the skills, temperament, energy and love to take on one of the most difficult jobs in the world – that of being a parent to a vulnerable child. It is a great feeling to have this endorsed!

The way panels are run is set down in regulations and guidance but there is variation about the detail in practice. Your social worker should explain the process that will apply in your case and the chairperson should also go over this with you.

You will normally leave the room while the panel members consider their recommendation, though some panels have applicants present while they have this discussion. You may be asked to wait until the panel has reached a conclusion and then invited back in to be advised what the panel intends to recommend. Or you may be advised that you will be contacted by phone by your social worker to let you know the outcome, either later in the day or as soon as possible. Panels usually reach a unanimous view about their recommendations, but occasionally there is a vote. Some agencies send applicants a copy of the minute taken at the panel.

Occasionally the panel might conclude that there is insufficient information to recommend that you should be approved and may defer a decision until this is rectified. This can be disappointing but the panel has to have all the information and evidence it needs to be able to make a recommendation, and this might involve you doing some more work with your social worker and coming back to a panel at a later date.

More rarely still, a panel might decide against recommending your approval, even though the social worker has recommended it.

The panel should be very clear with you about their reasons for this
and should provide a written explanation for you to consider.

The agency decision maker

Once the panel has arrived at a recommendation this will be
recorded in the minute and sent to the agency decision maker. The
role of the agency decision maker is to make a formal decision on
behalf of the agency about whether your application should be
approved. In the case of local authorities, the agency decision maker
also decides whether children should be adopted, who they should
be placed with and whether adoption allowances should be payable.
Usually the same agency decision maker will also make decisions
about the approval and review of foster carers. The agency decision
maker is usually a senior manager in the local authority. In the case
of VAAs, the role is sometimes given to a member of their Governing
Board who has relevant experience and some objectivity. The written
recommendation of the panel must be with the agency decision
maker within 14 days, and they have up to a further 14 days in
which to make a decision and write to the applicants.

The decision of the agency decision maker is the final link in the
chain of scrutiny and checks that are required under legislation to
ensure that the approval of adoptive parents has been given careful
consideration and complies with regulations, statutory guidance and
the policy of the agency. The whole process of approval might seem
onerous if you are not familiar with it, but it is important to stress
that for the majority of applicants the process is positive and even
enjoyable. It is necessary to safeguard the interests of vulnerable
children and the process needs to be rigorous.

What if you disagree with the decision of the agency?

If you do not agree with the decision of the adoption agency you should ask your social worker for details of the appeal process. The agency should have a procedure that sets down how this will be dealt with and how long it should take to consider. You will usually need to give your reasons for appealing in writing. This will be considered by the agency decision maker, who may consult with the panel chair and the manager of the adoption service. If the agency decision maker feels the agency has made the right decision he or she will let you know this. Sometimes the agency decision maker might ask for the matter to be looked at again, perhaps using an adoption panel with different members and a different chairperson. Occasionally the agency decision maker might ask a different agency or an independent person to look at the process to see if it was fair. If you remain dissatisfied after the appeal process has run its course, you can use the complaints procedure of the agency. It is not enough to appeal because you disagree with the decision: you need evidence to show why you believe the decision is wrong. No one has a *right* to adopt a child.

As well as going through the complaints procedure of the agency you can also consult the regulatory body – the Care Inspectorate. They can investigate complaints where the agency has not correctly adhered to appropriate procedures, or where professional standards have not been maintained. They cannot, however, overturn the agency decision.

5

Bringing children and families together: the matching and placement process

My life had not started off well, but as I am writing this story, events over the past seven years have changed my life forever.

Nine years ago I was put into foster care because my previous mum had been drinking alcohol and had been in trouble with the police. She had her chances to keep my brother and me, but she let us down time and again. I never knew how long I would be there for. The two years I was there seemed really long, I was always wondering when I would get my mum back again, but that never happened.

One day my social worker came to the house and informed us that they would be looking for a "forever" mum and dad for me and my brother. I spent most days intrigued about what they would be like and whether they would turn out to be like my old mum. We had settled into our foster home and I didn't want my brother and me to be put back into the same life we had escaped from two years earlier. I felt very excited but yet nervous at the same time. I was very relieved that my brother and I wouldn't be split up.

I now know, seven years down the line, that I didn't really know what the journey was going to be like, until now when I look back and I realise that all my fears were natural and the changes were for the better.

Meeting my mum and dad for the first time was very nerve-wracking because I didn't think they would like me. We went to the park on that first visit; it was good to share the excitement with the strangers that would become my mum and dad. Grant called them mum and dad on that first visit but I didn't feel ready yet. I still hoped that my "real" mum would come back and get me.

When we first moved in my brother was always testing my mum and dad by misbehaving. He finally started to settle down and realise that we had moved on and we have a new chance in life. Mum and dad bought us loads of new toys and clothes. We got to see all the other relatives. My new granny had made us a cake to welcome us to the family, but we never got a bit because we left and forgot about it. I always remember about that when I visit her. It always makes me laugh!

We moved house the first year we were with our new mum and dad, to a house instead of a flat. It was good not having to carry the messages to the top floor. I thought our house was one of the nicest in the street. I was glad to have my own room. We went on a surprise holiday to Corfu. We also have been to Florida three times. The most recent holiday we have been on was to the Dominican Republic and Florida with all the family including my gran, grandad, aunties, uncles and my cousin.

The things that were bought for us, and the holidays we have been on, aren't to boast. It is about my mum and dad working hard to be able to afford these nice things. Our family is all about respect and love for one another.

I wouldn't change the last seven years for all the money in the world because I have the best mum and dad ever.

Danny, aged 14

As outlined in the previous chapter, one of the functions of local authority adoption panels is to consider the needs of children. If the panel decides that the child needs to be adopted the child is sometimes referred to as being "registered" for adoption, though this is not a formal legal term. Most local authorities have children who are registered and waiting for adoption as well as other looked after children who have not yet been to the adoption panel but are likely to need adoption. Some local authorities have large numbers of children waiting for adoption whilst others have fewer.

There are a number of different ways in which adoptive parents are matched with children. The overriding consideration is always the needs of the child. The matching process is undertaken by the local authority adoption panel that has responsibility for the child. The formal matching meeting is usually preceded by a linking process.

The linking process

Once the local authority has identified one or more possible families who might be able to meet the needs of the child, they will usually convene a linking meeting. Sometimes more than one family is considered for a child at the linking meeting, particularly in relation to younger children, because there is more interest in them among adopters. The linking meeting is attended by the social worker for the child and the social workers for the adoptive families. It is usually chaired by a social work manager. Adoptive parents do not generally attend, but should be informed that the meeting is taking place. The meeting looks at how each family will meet the needs of the child and looks at factors such as geography, religion, ability to deal with particular health needs, etc. The views of the birth parents should be taken into account, for example in relation to religious upbringing. The child's agency must consider these views, but is not bound by them; the welfare of the child is paramount. A linking meeting will usually select a preferred family and a matching meeting of the adoption panel is then held, which has to make a recommendation to the agency decision maker.

The linking and matching process differs for adoptive families who have been approved by local authorities and those who have been approved by voluntary adoption agencies (VAAs), though there are similarities.

Local authorities

Each of Scotland's 32 local authorities is required by law to act as an adoption agency and as such has to arrange for the placement of children in need of adoption. Local authorities vary in terms of the areas they serve and the social problems they have to address. Broadly speaking, local authorities that cover urban areas have to deal with greater levels of social deprivation than those in rural parts of the country. Because of this, urban areas often have larger numbers of looked after children than rural ones, and also find it particularly challenging to recruit sufficient foster carers and adoptive parents to meet their needs. Some of the larger, urban authorities therefore have comparatively large numbers of children in need of adoption, in contrast to some rural authorities which have smaller numbers of children in need of adoption, but which find it easier to recruit adoptive families.

As a result of this mismatch in terms of where the adoptive parents live in Scotland and where the children in need of adoption come from, a number of local authorities have consortium arrangements; they work together to place children for adoption, or for permanent fostering. So, for example, a child in one local authority might be placed within another local authority that is a member of the same consortium. There are two major consortia in Scotland:

- **The West of Scotland Family Placement Consortium** is an arrangement between 12 local authorities and one voluntary adoption agency.
- **The North of Scotland Family Placement Consortium** is an arrangement between 10 local authorities.

Both of these consortia have formal arrangements for identifying children and adoptive parents so that they can be linked and potential matches explored.

In addition to these consortia, a number of other local authorities co-operate with each other in trying to find matches between adoptive families and children.

Scotland's Adoption Register

As well as the regional consortia, there is a Scottish Adoption Register, established in 2011, that links children in need of adoption with approved adoptive parents across Scotland by cross-matching the characteristics of each. It is sometimes used by local authorities that want to place children away from their local area to avoid unplanned contact with members of the birth family. It can also feature children that local authorities are finding hard to find families for, including sibling groups, children with disabilities or special needs and older children. There is a contrast between the profile of children referred to the register and the profile of approved adoptive families who are referred. In 2013, nearly two-thirds of children referred to the register were aged four and over, and nearly two-thirds of families referred were interested in adopting children *under* the age of four.

There is also an Adoption Register that covers England and Wales. Occasionally, children and families may be referred between the two registers. The Scottish Adoption Register is in its infancy and arrangements for this are still being developed. Both registers are currently run by the British Association for Adoption and Fostering (BAAF) under contracts with the respective governments. They are staffed by professional social workers, who carefully consider the needs of children and the profiles of families available and advise the social workers of the children of possible matches that might be appropriate. If it is agreed that a match might be viable with you, there will be further discussion and information sharing and you will then become directly involved.

Local authorities generally try to find a family that fits with the cultural needs of the child, and this usually means a placement in Scotland. Local authorities also have responsibilities to provide support to adoptive families, and this can be more easily achieved if the placement is reasonably local. However, some Scottish children are placed elsewhere in the UK. These are usually children with particular ethnic identities, or those who may be hard to place, such as children with certain disabilities. Similarly, some children from outside Scotland are placed here.

What can you expect after a local authority approves you as an adoptive parent?

If you have been approved by a local authority with high numbers of children waiting for adoption, your social worker might already have spoken to you about some of these children during your assessment process, and you may be linked with a child or children fairly quickly. If your profile does not fit with the children waiting for adoption you might have to wait longer. This can happen, for example, if you are black or have a particular ethnic profile and there are no children with a similar profile in need of adoption at that time. Or it may be that you have been approved for a very young child and the children waiting for adoption are older than this.

If the adoption agency is unable to link you with a child they may, with your agreement, refer you to one of the adoption consortia or to the Adoption Register. There may be children that match your profile in other parts of Scotland. Usually local authorities wait for a period of time after adoptive parents have been approved before referring them to the consortia or the Adoption Register. Local authorities will generally want to establish first if you can meet the needs of children for whom they are responsible, including children not yet born or children who may be looked after but are not yet available for adoption. There is currently no time scale within which local authorities are obliged to refer approved adoptive parents to the consortia or to Scotland's Adoption Register. However, if you have not had a child placed with you within one year of approval, there should be a review by the adoption panel, which will consider the reasons for this and will discuss options for the future. At this point the agency might suggest that you should be referred to the Adoption Register or to a consortium, if they have not already done so.

When social workers are considering links for children for whom they are trying to find an adoptive family, they will at some point have access to the assessment of the approved adoptive family and the minute of the adoption panel at which the family was approved. It is important that you ensure that both give a picture of you that you feel is accurate. Social workers seeking a link for a child will be influenced by how well-expressed your profile is. Spelling and grammar are not important but the profile needs to convey a sense of what it will be like for a child to be part of your family. Prospective adopters are often encouraged to compile albums of photographs and information, to assist social workers at the linking stage and to help adoption panels during the matching process. Sometimes families make DVDs of themselves and this is becoming more common as agencies look for creative ways of matching children with families.

If you have been approved by a voluntary adoption agency

Voluntary adoption agencies (VAAs) do not have formal responsibility for looked after children; their role in relation to adoption is to recruit adoptive families and to support them in caring for the children they adopt. They are dependent on the referral to them by local authorities of children in need of adoption. Some local authorities have contracts with VAAs, who as part of this arrangement will recruit a certain number of families per year for that local authority. Most children are, however, placed with a VAA as a result of a local authority referring a particular child, or through the Adoption Registers. If you have been approved by a VAA you can expect that your social worker will be active in trying to identify a child for you. It may be that the VAA knows of a child who would suit your profile before you are approved. VAAs and local authorities work closely in trying to meet the needs of children waiting for adoption. If there is no obvious link for you, you may be referred to Scotland's Adoption Register.

VAAs tend to have children that the local authority does not want to place locally or is finding it hard to recruit a family for. The profile of children *might* be more challenging than those placed by local authorities. They may, for example, have additional needs or a disability, or have experienced particular trauma and abuse and require a lot of patient care. Sibling groups are also difficult to place and can be referred to VAAs, as are children with particular ethnic profiles. Even though children placed with VAAs sometimes pose challenges, they tend to do very well; VAAs can provide good support and training to adoptive families and report very low rates of adoptions breaking down.

The law in Scotland means that at present only local authorities and voluntary adoption agencies can recruit adoptive families. Commercial agencies that seek to make financial gain are prohibited from recruiting adoptive parents or foster carers.

Finding your own child

Sometimes children are "advertised" as needing adoptive families. There are three main journals covering Scotland that carry profiles of children needing adoption.

Be My Parent

In the UK as a whole, the biggest journal is *Be My Parent*, published by BAAF, which features dozens of children waiting for adoption and fostering placements. The number of Scottish children featured tends to be small; usually only those who have not achieved a placement in Scotland or who have particular needs. You can see some of the children waiting for families by looking at the *Be My Parent* website (www.bemyparent.org.uk). In order to see all of the children waiting you need to subscribe to *Be My Parent*. You can receive hard copies of the magazine or an online version. You need to be an approved adoptive parent and you will need to be referred by your adoption agency. As well as profiling children waiting for adoption, *Be My Parent* also contains useful articles about adoption and fostering.

Scottish Children Waiting

This is produced by Scotland's Adoption Register, and contains profiles of children who have been referred to the Register's linking service. It contains details of between 30 and 50 children at any one time. There are photographs of many of the children featured. The publication is sent to all Scottish local authorities and voluntary adoption agencies, who in turn share it with approved adoptive parents.

Children Who Wait

This is a newsletter produced by Adoption UK, an agency established and run by adoptive parents. It features about 200 children across the UK at any one time, including a small number of Scottish children.

If you subscribe to any of the above journals and see the profile of a child who you feel might be a suitable match for you, it is best to discuss this with your social worker initially. They will talk over the potential match with you and get more information for you about the child if you agree this is appropriate.

National Adoption Week

During National Adoption Week (sponsored by BAAF each November) children may be profiled nationally on television and in newspapers. It is rare for Scottish children to be profiled in this way; there are legal complexities in advertising children unless the consent of the birth parents has been given, and in addition agencies have traditionally been cautious about exposing children in the media. Sometimes this media campaigning can lead to matches for children; approved adoptive parents might express interest after seeing a particular child featured, or people who have not thought previously about adoption might feel they could care for a profiled child and this might trigger an application from them. Sometimes, whilst the media exposure may not lead to a match for that particular child, it can start families thinking about adoption and lead eventually to the adoption of other children.

Adoption Information Exchange Days

In 2012 BAAF facilitated Information Exchange Days for the first time in Scotland. These provide an opportunity for approved adoptive families to find out more about some of the children waiting for adoption. A number of local authorities prepare profiles of children that include DVDs, pictures and stories by the children themselves, descriptions of the children compiled by foster carers and social workers, and other materials. The events tend to feature children who local authorities are finding it hard to find families for. The social workers, and some of the foster carers caring for the children are on hand to answer questions from prospective adopters. Children waiting for adoption do not attend. The events are open to approved adoptive parents who are waiting for children and around 40 attended the first event in Scotland. Many commented that it brought to life the profiles of children; it can be difficult to get a full picture of children based only on written information and discussions. Some adoptive parents went on to be matched with children who were outside the profile for which they were approved. On seeing the detailed profile of children who were a year or so older than that which the adoptive parents had thought they could manage, they reconsidered this, and the agency reviewed and amended the approval range. A number of matches were achieved as a result of these Information Exchange Days and it is planned that they will become a regular fixture, occurring perhaps twice a year.

Future developments

There are concerns in Scotland about the delay in finding adoptive families for children who need them. Efforts are being made to address this, with children being assessed more quickly, legal delays being tackled, more active recruitment of adoptive parents and new ways of matching children with approved adopters, such as the Information Exchange Days referred to previously. As a result of these efforts, there may be a rise in the proportion of younger children and infants who are available for adoption, though firm statistical information is not yet available. The number of adoptions in Scotland seems to be rising – there were 272 children adopted from care in 2012 compared to 264 the previous year and 218 in 2010. Agencies are looking at more creative ways of profiling children and finding families for them. As well as using the Information Exchange Days and the Scottish Adoption Register, adoption agencies are increasingly profiling children using DVDs, so that adoptive families can get more of a sense of the child and what they might be like to care for. Many adoption agencies now share real profiles of children with prospective adoptive parents before they are approved, or even at the first open evening, to help them decide if adoption is for them and to explore possible links at a very early stage. In other parts of the UK, agencies run Adoption Activity Days, where children waiting for adoption can be discretely seen by approved adopters. This approach has its critics; the notion of choosing a child out of a group of children might be seen as distasteful, and there is a concern to safeguard the dignity of children who might be involved in these events. These new techniques need to be considered if Scotland is to achieve lifelong families for children, and empower adoptive families to identify children who they might be able to parent.

Whatever method is used to profile children waiting for adoption, there is a need to support children who may not find an adoptive family and who will be feeling disappointed and distressed as a result.

Adopting children from a distance

If you are linked with a child who is cared for some distance away, you need to be sure that the placing local authority will provide the support you need. During the linking and matching process it is important that you find out what support will be available from your adoption agency/VAA, the local authority where you live if this is different, and the local authority which is responsible for the child. The question of support should be fully addressed, and you need to ensure that good plans are in place. The formal position in Scotland is that the placing local authority is responsible for supporting the adopted child for the first three years, and after that the local authority where you live becomes responsible (if this is different). Sometimes the placing local authority will negotiate with your local authority for support to be provided before the three years has elapsed. Most of the children placed from a distance are placed through Scottish VAAs, and they too will have a role in supporting the placement.

Some Scottish local authorities prefer not to place children too far away, so that they can provide good follow-up support to the children and families. Children placed from other parts of the UK might experience a cultural shift on coming to Scotland. However, VAAs report that these children do just as well as children placed locally. The most important thing is matching the child with a family that is best placed to meet their needs, and getting a good support package in place, including the availability of advice and personal support for the adoptive family.

The role of the adoption panel in matching children and families

Chapter 4 provided information about the role of the adoption panel in relation to the approval of adoptive parents. The adoption panel also has a role in matching approved adoptive parents with children.

After being approved as potential adopters, the waiting began!

I think that it is right that great care be taken over this, as it is a life-changing decision for all concerned! We were also realistic about the type of child that we felt that we could care for. I think that honesty is important here!

We had continued contact with social services and were fairly quickly identified as potential parents for a young boy. We were not successful and whilst we were disappointed, deep down we felt that the correct decision had been made!

We waited eight months from approval to the eventual placement of our children. I think that time does not matter. Putting the right child into the right family is more important.

Jane, adoptive parent of a sibling group of three

Once you have been linked to a child (or more than one) you will need to be formally matched by the adoption panel of the local authority with responsibility for the child, which then makes a recommendation to the agency decision maker. If you are being considered for a match with a child in the local authority that approved you, then this will be the same panel you attended when you were approved, though the panel members might be different. If the child is in the care of another local authority it will be that local authority's panel, not the one that approved you. If you were approved by a VAA then it will again be the panel for the local authority with responsibility for the child; this might be a Scottish local authority or one in a different part of the UK.

Practice varies in terms of whether adoptive parents are involved in matching panels. Some panels like to meet with prospective adopters whilst others involve only the social workers for the prospective adopters and the child. The panel will have before them all the papers relevant to the child. This will include a report (often using a template produced by BAAF known as Form E, although a Child's Adoption and Permanence Report template is being developed to replace this) which gives a history of the child and the birth family, and a comprehensive assessment of the child's needs. It includes medical information, hereditary issues, the history of the child's care, etc. You should have seen all of this information during the linking and pre-matching discussions. The panel will also have copies of your Form F, or whatever assessment framework was used, as well as the minute of the adoption panel that approved you, and any other relevant information. There should also be available any minutes of formal linking meetings that might have been held.

The panel will carefully consider all the information it has; this will have been circulated and read by panel members in advance. The social worker for the child will speak to the needs of the child, and your social worker will speak about how you will meet these needs. There will be a discussion that will consider whether the match should proceed.

Once the panel has reached a view, usually through consensus but occasionally through a vote, this is conveyed to the agency decision maker in the form of a minute of the panel with a formal recommendation. This also addresses questions such as whether an adoption allowance should be payable and may contain an outline of the Adoption Support Plan (see Chapter 8). The agency decision maker then makes a formal decision on behalf of the agency. You should normally be informed of the recommendation of the panel on the same day the panel meets, and you will get the agency decision maker's written report within a few days. As with the approval process, you can appeal against the decision if you are unhappy about it and believe the decision is wrong. If you feel the process of assessment and matching has been flawed, or the process has not been carried out as it should, you can complain to the agency or to the Care Inspectorate.

Introductions and moving in

The day a child moves into their placement is very special but it can also be complicated. Everyone can have high expectations – the day can have been months or even years in the planning, but emotions can be very mixed. For a start, the child will be experiencing a sense of excitement, but also of loss at leaving their foster carers – people who had been acting as parents up till then.

We attended preparatory groups and were assessed. The process took several months. It probably took about another six months to be matched with a child. We remember the first phone call to say there was a boy of three matched with us, and the range of emotions, from excitement, nervousness and anxiety that the wee boy would not like us, to worry that we were not as prepared as we thought we might be. There was a lot to go through before he was finally placed with us; planning meetings and visits from his foster carer and social worker. We also met with his birth mum before we met Sean. After that there was a series of planned visits in our home, then we got to take him out and then there was his first overnight stay with us. At last the day arrived when Sean came to stay for good. It must be up there with the best days of our lives and definitely near the top. It was a wonderful feeling to have this wee boy in our home and to care for him, something we had only dreamed about. That really was just the beginning.

Sarah and James, adoptive parents

After the matching meeting, sometimes immediately after, those who will be involved in introductions and the move of the child to your family will meet and discuss the next steps. You and the foster carers should be involved in this. Dates will be agreed as to when and where you will meet the child, and a timetable for moving in will be agreed. An Adoption Support Plan should be developed.

Robert and I made the first trip to the foster carers' house one Saturday. We'd met Mary, the female carer before, when we were finding out about William. She was a competent, confident woman. She greeted us warmly at the door and showed us into the living room. William was sitting in a special chair, meant to help him with his posture because of his disability. He had a little table in front of him and was playing with some toy trains. He turned as we came into the room and said, 'Hello, Mum and Dad.' He was all smiles. He'd been prepared for the meeting; it was clear that he was going to adopt us!

Evie, adoptive parent

The speed with which introductions proceed after you are matched with a child varies, depending on a number of factors. If there are no legal barriers, the introductions and placement might proceed very quickly.

We had an unusual situation where the foster carers had some personal issues and the children had to move quickly. So we met the children on the Saturday and then by the Wednesday they were living with us! It was a baptism of fire. But it was better than the children having to move to another foster care placement before they came to us. It seemed to work in our case. From the first day the kids were calling us mum and dad. We still keep in touch with the foster carers.

Lyndsay, adoptive parent

Assuming that you have not been involved in the care of the child previously, arrangements will be made for you to meet the child, usually in the foster carers' home or on neutral ground. The child will have been prepared for this meeting. If they are of an age to understand what is happening, the notion of finding a *forever* family through adoption will have been explained to them by their social worker and foster carers. Life story work should have been undertaken with them. This helps them make sense of why they are not living with their birth parents, and children usually have a book or album with photographs, pictures and stories that summarise events in their lives and try to explain these.

The child might move in with you within days, though a period of a few weeks is more usual. During this time there will be a series of meetings for you and the child to get to know each other and for you to find out the child's routines and needs in detail. It is an exciting time, a hectic time and sometimes a scary time. All those months, sometimes years, of preparation and detached discussions and suddenly here you are with a real child in front of you who is about to move in, and a whole host of feelings to contend with. But just think about what it is like for the child! They too will have mixed feelings – 'At last here is my forever family who I have been waiting for for so long. But hang on, they do things differently from my foster carers; they don't look like I imagined them; they talk funny; their house is too tidy; they smell odd; I don't like the soap they use; this food isn't what I'm used to. Why don't I love them? I'm going to miss my foster carers. It's a long way away…'

The adoption training started in January and took around six months. By August we had been accepted as prospective adoptive parents by the adoption panel. We were so pleased with the speed we were trained at and how quick the panel were able to make a decision. In October two children were matched with us and the plan was for them to join us in the following January – just 12 months from starting the adoptive journey we were to have two little ones in our lives!

It was actually late February when our two came to us. We had to foster them initially because the legal process of adoption hadn't been completed. The handover period from the former foster carers was short. This helped the children, as it was difficult for them to say goodbye, but it left us in a whirlwind! How strange must it have been for them to start anew again? We, however, were just stunned. The children were five and six and we had to hit the ground running, continuing their already established routine and learning about their personalities – who they really are.

Keeping their routine and not changing their nursery and school were key to them both settling in well. Of course we had dozens of questions from them to deal with all at once – most of which we had no answers to initially! We had our questions too, but most of those answered themselves as weeks turned into months and we began to gel as a family.

Our two were desperate to make attachments, but these for a while were formed at a superficial level. They had a mistrust of grown-ups as there had been no consistency of any one adult in their early years.

Three years on and I'm more certain than ever that we made the right decision to adopt. They have slotted into our lives so well, as well as with their many cousins in the extended family.

At times we rue the loss of our quiet days and weekend lazy lie-ins, but we both agree that our two have brought fun and a richness of life that we could have never anticipated.

Bruce, adoptive parent

Introductions and placement can be slower if the child is subject to certain legal proceedings. In some cases the permission of the Children's Hearing and the court needs to be obtained before a child can move into the adoptive family, and this can sometimes take weeks or even months. This is plainly not in the best interests of the child and local authorities try to find ways to reduce these delays wherever possible. Whilst delays in the placement of children can be reduced, the legal process can still take time.

I have two sons, one now aged 11 and one who is eight. Lewis, the older one, was placed with us at the age of 22 months and his adoption went through six months later. The following May we were approached by social work services and asked if we would be interested in adopting Lewis's brother, and Joey moved in with us in June, when he was just four days old. However, the adoption process took much longer for Joey; it was nearly three years before it was completed. That was difficult because Joey's birth mother was still seeing him and was contesting the adoption, and it took time for the court and the Children's Hearing to make a final decision. But it did mean that Joey came to us without having been in other care placements, so the bonding with him was

easier. The legal process is behind us now and we are really
happy and have sheer pleasure and delight in the wonderful
life that we now have.

Shona, adoptive parent

Meeting birth parents

It is fairly common these days for adoptive parents to meet the birth
parents before the child is placed. There are a number of reasons
why this can be helpful for all parties. The birth parents might be
anxious or distressed at the prospect of their child going to live with
another family for life. Meeting the adoptive parents can be
reassuring and can help them to know that the child will be safe and
well cared for. The meeting can also give adoptive parents a real
sense of who the birth parents are, and this can be shared with the
child as he or she grows up. The meeting can be important, too, in
reassuring the child that the birth parents were, to a degree, involved
in the process; they wanted to meet the child's new parents and they
wanted the best for the child. Sometimes other important figures in
the child's life, such as grandparents, meet with the adoptive
parents. Any meetings are supervised by the child's social worker and
sometimes the adoptive family's social worker too. The meetings are
on neutral ground and are carefully managed.

Sometimes there might be a contact arrangement between the child
and the birth family. This usually involves indirect contact, including
the exchange of letters and perhaps photographs once a year.
Occasionally there might be ongoing direct contact with the birth
family. Any contact needs to be in the best interests of the child: if
there are indications that contact is not helpful it should be
reviewed, and might subsequently be reduced or ceased.

It can sometimes be important to keep in touch with foster carers or
other important figures such as siblings.

My adopted son has two birth brothers who are adopted and we all get together a couple of times a year. As soon as they meet they seem to connect emotionally, even though they have never lived together. It feels very important for them all.

Evie, adoptive parent

6

The legal process

Formal adoption in Scotland was first developed in the 1930s. Before this, adoption was arranged on a private basis, either by individuals or by charitable organisations, with little state involvement. The Adoption of Children (Scotland) Act 1930 introduced legal adoption. Adoption was seen then as a solution for unwanted babies at a time when it was socially unacceptable to have children out of wedlock. At the same time, adoption provided a service for childless married couples. Since then, adoptions have continued to be facilitated by voluntary organisations and also by local authorities, with the courts playing a role in ratifying adoptions through a legal process.

Adoption in the modern sense was developed by the 1978 Adoption (Scotland) Act and there were further developments with the Adoption and Children (Scotland) Act 2007, when adoption by same-sex couples was legalised and different processes for achieving adoption for children were introduced.

The possibility that adoption might offer children in public care the opportunity of being brought up as part of a family was first developed in the United States. It was later taken up in the UK, and in Scotland small numbers of children were adopted from care in the 1960s and onwards. The practice continued in the 1970s and 1980s, when, as birth control improved and the stigma of being a lone parent largely disappeared, there were fewer babies available for adoption than previously, but large numbers of children being brought up in care. The challenge of parenting these children is quite different from parenting a baby who would be placed with the adopters direct from hospital or after a short placement with foster carers.

The legal process of adopting a child varies across the country because of the way practice has developed in different courts and local authorities. However, the process can broadly be divided into three stages. Stage 1 involves getting approved by an adoption agency as an adoptive parent. Stage 2 involves linking, matching and placing children – in other words identifying one or more children for you to adopt and moving them into your family. The third, and final, stage of the legal process is the granting by the court of an Adoption Order, which transfers the rights and responsibilities for the care of the child to you, as the child's new parents. A summary of the three stages is given below.

Stage 1
Getting approved

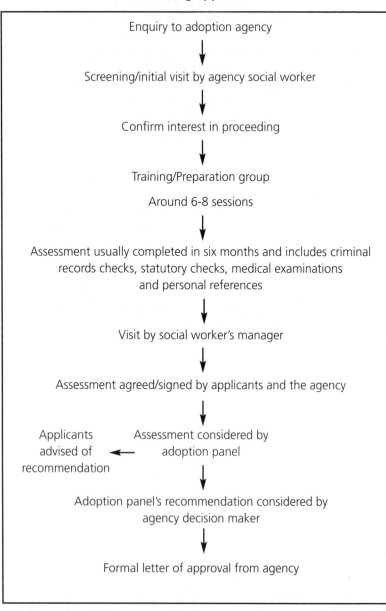

Enquiry to adoption agency

↓

Screening/initial visit by agency social worker

↓

Confirm interest in proceeding

↓

Training/Preparation group

Around 6-8 sessions

↓

Assessment usually completed in six months and includes criminal
records checks, statutory checks, medical examinations
and personal references

↓

Visit by social worker's manager

↓

Assessment agreed/signed by applicants and the agency

↓

Applicants   Assessment considered by
advised of   ◄—   adoption panel
recommendation

↓

Adoption panel's recommendation considered by
agency decision maker

↓

Formal letter of approval from agency

Stage 2
Linking and matching process with child(ren)

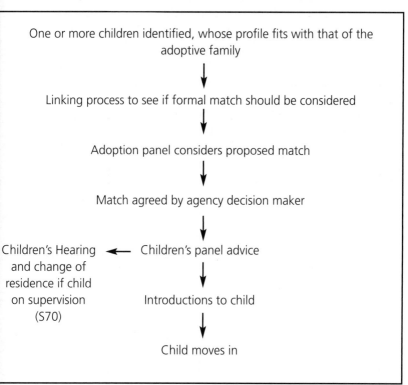

One or more children identified, whose profile fits with that of the adoptive family

↓

Linking process to see if formal match should be considered

↓

Adoption panel considers proposed match

↓

Match agreed by agency decision maker

↓

Children's Hearing and change of residence if child on supervision (S70) ◄— Children's panel advice

↓

Introductions to child

↓

Child moves in

Stage 3
The court process in granting an Adoption Order

The adoptive applicants/solicitor apply to the court for Adoption Order

---

If the child subject to a Permanence Order with Authority to Adopt (POA), the process should now be straightforward

↓

Court asks for reports and sets a date for a hearing

↓

Curator ad litem visits adoptive family and writes report

↓

Private court hearing

↓

Adoption Order granted

If the child is on a Compulsory Supervision Order the legal process can be more complicated

↓

Court gets advice from the Children's Hearing

↓

Court sets date to hear case and gets reports from the local authority about the suitability of the adoptive applicants and the circumstances of the child

↓

If the case is contested by the birth parents, the court hears evidence in private from both sides

↓

Court gets reports from Curator ad litem and Reporting Officer

↓

Court considers evidence – may take some time

↓

Adoption Order granted

In order to adopt a child so that they become *your* child, you have to make an application to a court following the process outlined in stage 3 above.

The law can feel complicated and off-putting and you must not feel overwhelmed by this. It is there to help and protect everyone, and the needs of the child have to be at the centre. When you go through the court process you will have a solicitor to help you, and the adoption agency will give you support, but it can also be useful for adoptive parents to know how children become looked after, and what this means for the child and those caring for them.

The Children's Hearing system

Scotland has laws that are quite distinct and different from other parts of the UK. The courts also have different names and different powers. Decisions about the care and wellbeing of children in Scotland are generally made by a system known as the Children's Hearing system. This is not a type of court, but is underpinned by the courts in certain circumstances. The Children's Hearing system has paid officials known as Children's Reporters. Reporters usually have qualifications in law or social work. The role of the reporter is to receive referrals about children whose welfare is causing concern, and to decide whether a Children's Hearing should be called to consider if compulsory measures of care are needed. Children are usually referred to the Children's Hearing system either because there are concerns about their care and protection, or because they have got into trouble with the police.

The Children's Hearing itself (sometimes called a children's panel) is a meeting attended by panel members who are responsible for making decisions about the care and supervision of the child. The National Convenor of Children's Hearings Scotland is responsible for the recruitment, appointment and reappointment of panel members under the provisions of Children's Hearings (Scotland) Act 2011. Children's Hearings cannot decide points of law – if these are in question they have to be decided by a court.

Children who are relinquished by their parents

A small number of children are still voluntarily relinquished for adoption by their birth parents. They include children born as a result of unplanned pregnancies, whose mothers may be very young or whose circumstances are such that they have decided that they do not wish to be parents at this time. Sometimes such pregnancies might be concealed right up to the point of birth. Mothers choosing to relinquish their babies are always offered counselling by the local authority or by a voluntary agency to help them be sure that this is the step they wish to take. Sometimes they change their mind during this process. Occasionally older children might also be relinquished for adoption in this way.

The number of relinquished babies and children in Scotland is small. It is easy to find adoptive families for such babies, who are occasionally available for adoption straight after birth. They are sometimes placed with prospective adopters on leaving hospital.

The adoption of *any* child is not wholly straightforward, even babies placed straight from hospital. The paternity of the baby may not be known, and the adopters will have to explain this to the child one day and face questions such as why the birth mother did not want to care for them. The legal process in relation to relinquished children is fairly uncomplicated, but there are some uncertainties. The court cannot grant an Adoption Order until the child is at least 19 weeks old and has been in the care of the prospective adoptive parents for at least 13 weeks. These timescales apply to *all* adoptions. This gives the court time to judge if the adoptive placement is likely to be successful, and it gives the birth parent time to be sure they are making the right decision.

All decisions about adoption are ultimately made by courts. Some legal processes involving the adoption of children are straightforward and others are more complicated. Put in its simplest form, birth parents either consent to adoption or they do not. If they do not consent, the local authority sometimes applies to the sheriff court for a Permanence Order with Authority to Adopt (POA), or they can ask the adopters to apply to the court to adopt the child. Whichever route is taken, adopters always have to make a court application before the Adoption Order can be granted.

Social workers in local authorities cannot simply decide that a birth parent should not care for their child. Even if there are serious concerns about the care of that child, the local authority needs to obtain powers through the Children's Hearing system or the courts to remove the child from the care of their parents or guardian against their wishes and place the child elsewhere. The local authority has a duty to consider whether any close relatives may be in a position to care for a child who cannot be cared for by his or her birth parents.

A child placed with you for adoption will probably either be the subject of a POA or will be on supervision through the Children's Hearing system.

The process for adopting a child who is the subject of a POA

A POA is an order made by the court (usually the sheriff court). Only a local authority can make an application for a POA. The local authority has to prove that the child's birth parents are not able to meet the needs of the child and that the child needs to be adopted. In granting a POA, the court gives the local authority full parental responsibilities for the child, including the power to place them with adoptive parents. The birth parents no longer have any rights and responsibilities and do not need to be consulted any more.

If a child is placed with you on a POA the court process you have to follow to adopt the child is straightforward. You fill in an application form to adopt the child. This is obtained from your local sheriff court. A solicitor can do all this for you if you need help, or the adoption agency can advise. You can make this application any time after the child has been placed with you, but, as mentioned above, the court cannot grant an Adoption Order until the child is at least 19 weeks

old and has lived with you for at least 13 weeks. The court will set a
date to hear your application, and will appoint someone called a
Curator ad litem, who is usually a solicitor or a social worker. They
will prepare a report for the court in relation to your adoption
application. The report will give the views of the child if they are able
to express them. The court cannot agree to the adoption of a child
over the age of 12 unless the child consents. The report will say how
the child is settling in with you and will recommend whether
adoption by you is in the child's best interests.

---

*The court appointed a lawyer who visited us in our home and
interviewed us and then the children. He also inspected the
house to make sure that it was suitable for the children. I am
not houseproud – our home was simply clean and in
reasonable order! It is not so now!*

Jane, adoptive parent

The court hearing is usually a formality. You and the child can go
along to the hearing. Sometimes the sheriff will talk to you and the
child about the adoption.

---

*Eventually the sheriff in chambers granted the Adoption
Order. We took the children with us to court. The sheriff had
three children of his own and wished us the best of luck!*

Jane, adoptive parent

Many adoptive parents like to have some sort of record of the day,
perhaps a photograph outside the court or even with the sheriff (it
does no harm to ask if he or she will agree to this!).

---

*We went to court in the July. It was a lovely experience. My
mum and dad came along, as did my link worker and*

Cameron's social worker, to share the moment. The sheriff was lovely and it was all very relaxed. He played with Cameron and gave him sweets, then congratulated me on my new son. Tears all round!!

Fiona, single adoptive parent

Once the court has agreed to the adoption application they will contact the Registrar General for Scotland. The child's original birth certificate will be removed from the national records and you will be sent an amended certificate naming you as the adoptive parents.

If you are adopting a child who is subject to a POA, you are unlikely to have contact with the birth parents at court – they will normally have ceased to be involved in the process when the POA was granted.

The costs associated with adopting a child who is subject to a POA are small. Sometimes the local authority will meet these costs.

The process for adopting a child who is subject to a Compulsory Supervision Order (CSO)

If the child placed with you is subject to supervision through the Children's Hearing (a CSO), the case for adoption will not yet have been proved in court, though the local authority will be confident that there is enough evidence for this. In order to care for a child who is on a CSO, i.e. who is looked after (in care), you will have to be approved as foster carers as well as adoptive parents by your agency's adoption and fostering panel.

To adopt a child who is on a CSO, you will need a solicitor who will have to make an application to the court on your behalf. This is called a direct petition. This just means that you, not an adoption agency, are initiating the application. The court will get a report from the local authority which describes you as a family, outlines the circumstances of the child and sets out how you will meet the child's needs. The court will set a date to hear the application. Your solicitor will present the evidence to show the court that the child needs to be adopted, including information and records of the adoption panel that decided that the child needed to be adopted. If the birth parents do not agree to the adoption they have a right to present their case in court. They will need to persuade the court that they are able to care for the child. Sometimes birth parents will not give consent to the adoption, but when it comes to the court process they do not oppose the application. If they do oppose the adoption application in court they will usually have a solicitor to help them.

When your solicitor presents the case for adoption, he or she will usually call the birth parents as witnesses, and will ask them questions about their past care of the child, their history and lifestyle, to demonstrate that they are not in a position to care for the child. You may also have to give evidence, mainly about what you are like as a family and how the child is settling in with you. Other people, including the child's social worker, may also have to give evidence. This will be about why the child's birth parents are unable to care for the child, in order to demonstrate that the child needs to be adopted.

The birth parents' solicitor will also call witnesses and might cross-examine you and the other witnesses. The process can take several days, after which the sheriff will consider the case for a time before giving a judgement.

At last Sean was adopted and legally ours. We celebrated that day, we cried, laughed and held him so tight. Sean took it in his stride and went out to play. The difference that piece of paperwork made was great: we all relaxed more and it was good to be able to live without the constant coming and going of social workers, lawyers and other appointments.

Sarah, adoptive parent

The prospect of a complex legal process can seem a bit daunting, but remember that the local authority will have taken legal advice along the way and will be confident that there are strong grounds for adoption. By the time you get to court you will have had the care of the child for some time, and there should be strong evidence that they are settling in your care and making good progress. This will positively influence the sheriff, because it shows that adoption by you is in the child's interests. This is usually in stark contrast to the child's experience of care when they were living with their birth parents.

There is less legal certainty for children being adopted through a direct petition than there is for children being adopted who already have a POA. The reasons local authorities sometimes encourage adoptive parents to make direct petitions is that it can mean that children are placed with their forever family sooner, and therefore at a younger age.

The local authority with responsibility for the child will usually meet all the legal costs associated with a direct petition.

If the case for adoption is likely to be difficult to prove, the local authority will probably have chosen to apply for a POA first. This will mean that you, as adoptive parents, will not have to deal with an uncertain legal process after taking over the care of the child.

The vast majority of direct petitions are successful, but there is always a small chance that the court will not agree to the adoption. Even if the court does not agree to the adoption, the child will stay in your care because they will be on a Compulsory Supervision Order, with a requirement that they should live with you. In this case the local authority will have a meeting to consider what should happen next.

Caring for a child who is on a CSO

During the time the child is subject to a CSO, and is waiting for the legal adoption process to be completed, the Children's Hearing system has an ongoing role in ensuring the arrangements for the care of the child are meeting their needs. If you are caring for a child on a CSO you might have to go along to Children's Hearings. The birth parents may also attend these hearings. If there are likely to be difficulties about this for you, arrangements can be made so that you do not have contact with them. Your address can be kept from the birth parents if need be.

The Children's Hearing will be asked to give views to the court about the proposed adoption. The Children's Hearing also has to make decisions about whether the birth parents of the child should have contact with them until the question of adoption has been decided.

Permanence Orders and Residence Orders

Adoption is the only true form of permanent care in that it transfers all rights and responsibilities to the new adoptive parents and is intended to promote the child's best interests throughout life. It gives the child a right to inherit property and the adoptive parents will always be the child's legal parents. Sometimes other legal measures are also described as permanent arrangements. The Permanence Order is one such measure. It is granted by a court and the child remains looked after until the age of 18, but is not supervised through the Children's Hearing system. Another is the Residence Order, commonly referred to as Section 11. This is an order, usually granted by a sheriff, which transfers parental responsibilities to the applicant. The court decides which responsibilities should be part of the order. The birth parents retain some responsibilities. Children who are subject to a Residence Order are *not* looked after by the local authority. Residence Orders are most commonly used when relatives seek the care of children, but can occasionally be used in relation to children in foster care. The local authority has the power to pay an allowance to those caring for such children. The Residence Order lasts until the child is 16.

Intercountry adoption

People wishing to adopt a child from another country have to be assessed and approved as suitable to adopt by an adoption agency in the UK. In Scotland this application then has to be endorsed by the Scottish Government. The matching process is undertaken by the country where the child lives. Once the child is in the care of the prospective adopters in Scotland an application is made by them to the court in the same way as for other adoptions.

Non-agency adoptions

Non-agency adoptions include adoptions by step-parents and close relatives. The prospective adoptive parents do not have to be approved by an adoption agency. The prospective adopters do, however, have to let their local authority know that they intend to apply to adopt the child. A social worker from the local authority will then need to investigate and provide a report to the court (commonly called a Section 19 report). This gives information about the circumstances of the adoption and has to report on whether the adoption will meet the child's needs throughout his or her life.

7

Understanding your adopted child: an introduction to attachment theory

All children who are in need of adoption will have had a difficult start in life. Many will consequently need extra help from their adoptive parents in learning how to trust people and make positive relationships. An essential ingredient in the healthy development of children is that they experience sensitive care from those who look after them. This sensitive care helps children to develop positive attachments to their parents, and this is an important foundation for growing up into healthy, happy, well-adjusted adults, able to deal with the challenges of life and able to enjoy friendships and intimate relationships.

If you are thinking of adopting a child, it is important to understand how children learn to form positive attachments. You need to know what can happen if children have not received sensitive care, and you need to think about the challenges that might be involved in caring for such children.

Our adoption experience hasn't been easy, but each day you get something back and that keeps you going. One of the most monumental experiences I had still gets me emotional when I think about it. Peter's head had been held under water when his birth mother tried to drown him, so obviously bath times were very traumatic. We spent a lot of time carefully giving him toys and encouraging him in the bathroom to help him feel less anxious about it. Teaching him to swim was a huge step. I remember going along to the swimming baths thinking, 'I am going to get flung out of here because this child is screaming', and walking up and down, but then getting enough confidence to say to myself, 'Do you know what pal, I don't care if you are staring at me, or what you think I am doing, I am doing this for my child and you can stare if you like!' Eventually it paid off and Peter gradually started to put his own face under the water. I kept my distance, to give him his space, staying back and letting him do it. When he swam for the first time it was overwhelming.

One time he hurt himself and needed help in the bath. He'd cut his arm. He was about eight years old by then, so he usually bathed himself and I'd just leave the door open and be around and give him a bit of privacy. But because he had hurt his arm I was in there to help him. So there I was, chatting away to him, but still being very mindful about his fear of water, even after all those years. I was kneeling back and chatting with him and I said, 'Right we need to do your hair.' I'd brought a jug up with me on purpose and I said, 'I'll pour it over your head,' and he said, 'No, no, no, I will do it myself,' and whoosh, he lay back. That was the way he had been held under water all that time ago. I thought, 'Oh my God, he has lain back in the water.' He got back up and shampooed his hair and I said, 'I'll use the jug to rinse it if you like,' and he said, 'No, no, no I'll do it.' He goes back down into the water and the soap is all floating at his head, so I am pointing at him and saying, 'You need to get that bit,' but he says, 'No, you

*do it.' Then I had my hands on his head in a bath of water,
and I just cried. I rinsed his hair and I said, 'Right son,' and I
got him out and came down the stairs and sat and just
bawled my eyes out. I said, 'I can't believe that that wee boy
has got enough trust in me to have my hands on his head
under the water.'*

Ann, adoptive parent

What is attachment?

Attachment describes the bond between a child and his or her
parents or main carers. From birth and through childhood,
particularly early childhood, children behave naturally in ways that
attract the attention of their parents, so that their parents will
protect, comfort and care for them. When babies are tired or hungry,
uncomfortable or afraid, they cry and thrash about and are soothed
when the parent responds positively by meeting their needs. The
parent develops a bond with the child that will have started at the
point of birth when the baby first emerges into the world (or even
before this) and is held closely. The attachment of the child to the
parent develops over time in response to the interaction between the
child and the parent. Most children develop secure attachments.
Their parents are sensitive to their needs and provide dependable
care, so the child knows they can rely on them. Such children are
more likely to grow up feeling confident, with a good sense of self-
esteem, and an ability to make positive relationships and deal with
problems without getting upset or angry.

The development of secure attachments is not the only factor that
shapes the way we develop as individuals, but it is very important.
Other things that influence the way we turn out as adults include
hereditary factors and temperament, stresses we might experience in
life, and the support and interaction we have with people other than
our parents, such as teachers and relatives. Even some children who
do have secure attachments with their parents can have problems in

later life. The way we develop as people is complicated and influenced by all sorts of factors.

There are a number of different styles of attachment that children develop. Secure attachment, as mentioned above, is the one most likely to lead to positive development. The style least likely to lead to positive development is known as disorganised attachment.

What is disorganised attachment?

Children are most likely to develop this type of attachment if their parents or carers are not sensitive to their needs and do not provide consistent care. The result of this is that the child does not know how the parent is going to react to his or her needs and does not therefore learn how to communicate their needs clearly. Some studies into attachment show that around 15 per cent of all children develop this type of disorganised attachment style, and around 80 per cent of children who have been maltreated may have attachment difficulties. The attachment style develops over a period of time. It is largely shaped in the first three years of life but carries on developing throughout childhood.

Difficulties with attachment can be significant for children being placed for adoption. They may have experienced neglect, inconsistent parenting or maltreatment by their birth parents, on top of which they may have been looked after by a succession of carers before being placed for adoption, so that there will have been inconsistency in the care they received. These children therefore need sensitive caring by their adoptive parents, who need to work hard in providing the love and consistency they need to maximise the chances that they will grow into happy well-adjusted adults. Some children respond well to this but others remain challenging to care for.

The needs of children

When a baby is born, they are very dependent on those around them to meet all their needs. All babies need to have their physical needs met. Their early behaviours, such as crying when something is not right, are designed to keep their parents close by, so that they can protect the child. They need to be fed, kept warm and clean. They also need to be loved: they need to be held, rocked, sung and talked to. The smell of their parents is familiar, and this and other things they recognise about the parents makes them feel secure. They can recognise the way their parents hold them, they know their voices and they respond to this by feeling soothed and comforted. Good quality parenting is reliable and responsive as well as sensitive to the needs and demands of the infant, and helps to develop a secure attachment between the child and the parents.

As the child develops, the bond with their parents gets closer, and the child develops a sense of safety and security that equips them to explore the world. The child knows they are loved. They know the parents will meet their need for food, comfort and love, and that they will always be there and keep them safe. But even children who are brought up in loving families have vulnerability. If mum is unexpectedly not there when needed the child can get distressed; if she does not respond quickly enough to crying, the crying will increase. That first separation at nursery, with a childminder or at school can be distressing, until the child is reassured that the parent will come back and still loves them. Even so, children can "punish" their parents by, for example, not returning affection or by having a tantrum when they have been separated or their needs have not been met in the way they expected. Without love, or with love that is unreliable or unpredictable, babies and children get confused and do not develop the sense of security they need.

Parenting is a difficult job. Many people grow up in families where attachment with parents is not altogether reliable. We all have our different personality traits, emotional vulnerabilities and ways of behaving that we know are not quite as we would like them to be,

but which we cannot do a lot about. Most people find ways of coping with who they are and are able to interact with others in a way that gets them through life and achieves a state of happiness for much of the time.

Children who are in need of adoption will have experienced inconsistent care beyond the usual range. It is rare for babies to be placed with prospective adopters at birth, but even those who are may have missed out on immediate skin-to-skin contact at birth which, for other babies, is the beginning of the attachment bonding with the parents.

Some studies show that without attachment to a parent figure in the early weeks and months of life, a baby's brain does not develop as it does in other children. Brain scans taken of children show that those who have been brought up in loving families where their emotional needs have been met appropriately have different, more complete brain development, than those brought up without their emotional needs being properly met. Studies of children who were brought up in large orphanages in Eastern Europe, and who spent a significant amount of their time in closely-packed beds and cots, show that the children whose brain development was most impaired had had the least contact with people who could give them affection. The numbers of care staff were too low to enable them to give much time to individual children. The children who were closest to the doors, and hence had some contact with cleaning staff and other auxiliary staff, had better brain development than those children furthest away from the doors and who therefore had less contact with anyone who could give them attention or affection.

Children in need of adoption will have a variety of histories, often very complicated ones. They may have been born into chaotic families with parents who used drugs or alcohol, and who as a result provided them with inconsistent care. Their parents may have genuinely loved them, but not been able to prioritise the needs of their child over other matters. Or they may have had addiction problems that superseded other considerations. Intermittent love is not enough to ensure that a child develops healthily. If the child is given good care one day, with lots of attention, stimulation and love, but the next day the parent cannot get out of bed to feed them when they are hungry, or is unable to smile at them and give them attention, the child becomes confused and does not know what to expect. Prolonged exposure to inconsistent care or maltreatment can lead to severe problems in terms of the ability to trust others, a sense of self-esteem and even the development of intelligence.

Sometimes children in need of adoption have not only experienced very inconsistent care from their birth parents, but have also been physically or sexually abused. Often we do not know the full story of the child's history and the experience they might have had. The way we, as humans, deal with stress is partly regulated by the release of hormones. This release can become disturbed in maltreated children, so that their responses to stressful events may not be the same as for other children, sometimes long after they have been placed in positive care settings. They may, for example, deny having done something wrong, even though the evidence is blindingly obvious! They may become unreasonably angry or frustrated when something does not go the way they expect. They may be prone to temper tantrums. They might find it difficult to form close relationships. Children with histories of maltreatment might make superficial relationships and be over-friendly towards strangers and people they hardly know.

We have all had experience of trauma at some point in our lives. Think of a loss or shock you have had; maybe the death of someone you love, an experience of losing your job, failing an important examination, realising your partner has been unfaithful or falling out with someone you were close to. Such experiences can trigger acute distress and the process of recovery can be painful, even for those of us who are surrounded by dependable relationships, have learned how to manage our feelings maturely, and who have high self-esteem and belief in ourselves. Now imagine how a child might deal with the trauma of abuse or separation from their parents, particularly if she or he has not developed an ability to manage their feelings and does not have a sense of security. Think how it must feel for a child who does not yet have verbal skills and the ability to reason things out.

Nurture over nature

They tell me that I hid, when we first met, behind a chair;
I was young and had not yet learnt to trust others.

A small boy, my brother, rushing forward delighted.
New people. A man and a woman. You were both nervous, I think.
Did I smile at you?
No, probably not. He did though; my brother was fine.

I was moved around a lot.
Was it strange? Upsetting?
I don't know. I don't think that I can remember; not any more.
From a mother who could not be a mother,
To parents who were not mine and were not to be mine,
And eventually to you:
To my parents who were not my parents
And yet were to be mine for the rest of my life.

Strange?
Yes.

But even lacking trust as I did,
Something must have sparked a small flame in my heart and in yours.
You both came back for us didn't you?

Thank you.

From the darkness of the night that could only be described as my past,
You two managed to light the candle that is my life; that is my future.

Hannah, aged 16 (adopted at five years old)

The care system sometimes compounds attachment difficulties. Few children in need of adoption are placed with their adoptive parents straight from home or hospital. They will usually have been placed with foster carers on an emergency basis, often with little preparation, because that is the way problems come to light. The social work service might have been contacted following a crisis when the child was found unattended or had been abused. There is the trauma of separation from their parents for the child. Then, often, there is uncertainty about the future plan for the child while an assessment is made about whether they can return home or whether there might be relatives who can provide care. Commonly, the initial foster carers cannot provide care other than for a short period, so the child has to be moved to other foster carers. Sometimes, the child goes home after the parents have been able to make changes to their lifestyle and have responded to the concerns that have been raised about the care of the child, only for the child to have to be re-admitted to care later. The process of assessing the child's needs, the potential of their parents or other members of the family to care for them, and planning for the future can take months or even years.

Given all this, it is surprising that children are not more damaged than they seem. Children can be remarkably resilient and can recover from trauma and develop positive attachments, given the right care and understanding. Even the brain can regain some of the growth that might have been impaired in the early stages of development and IQ can be increased.

We were expecting a really difficult time when our children were placed. The social worker described someone like Damien from the films, but it wasn't like that; it has been much better than we ever expected. I guess social workers want to prepare you for the worst to make sure you are prepared and are going to stick with it…

After they'd been with us for a while it was fantastic the first time that the two of them turned around and said, 'I love you,

Daddy,' without being prompted. That one moment where you don't prompt them and it is natural. I think I was doing something on the iPad and they just turned around and said, 'I love you Daddy.' 'What are you looking for?' I asked. 'Oh nothing, I just love you,' and then they just toddled out of the kitchen. I cook the breakfast at the weekend and they come into the kitchen and they want to be with me. They will sit up on the counter tops and listen to the music that I listen to, rather than Carly Rae Jepsen's "Call Me Maybe" for the seventh time. They listen to my music and they just want to be with me, and that is the reward that makes it worthwhile.

Gordon, adoptive parent

For children who are living in circumstances where they receive poor quality parenting, the damage can, to a degree, be offset if they have other attachment figures in their life. There may, for example, be grandparents or other relatives who provide some stability and who give positive attention to the child. The child might get some experience of positive care from a childminder or nursery or from a teacher. These positive experiences can be very important in helping the child's emotional development.

Foster carers play an important role in addressing some of the developmental gaps that children might have experienced. Consistent, reliable care can help children to catch up, and often those who have been neglected or maltreated can blossom when placed with foster carers. For such children who go on to be adopted there is the trauma of a further separation from these same carers, but many children can successfully transfer their growing ability to form positive attachments to the new adoptive parents. Even if a child is in foster care for a short period before moving on to an adoptive placement or a longer-term foster placement, it is important that they are given a positive, loving experience. Whilst this might mean that there will be a loss for the child when they move on, it is healthier for them to have a positive relationship, and to experience pain at separation, than not to have their emotional needs met by a foster carer.

Parenting a child with attachment difficulties

*When we first met our adopted son, before he was placed
with us, his first words were 'Hello Mum and Dad!' though
we obviously had no relationship with him at that time. We
believe he is now securely attached to us, but it probably took
around two years before we felt we genuinely loved him and
he loved us. Now that he is a young adult, issues relating to
his early attachment difficulties are still common. He finds it
difficult to say goodbye. He finds separation hard – if he goes
away for a weekend he is usually unwell when he comes
back. He can be totally irrational and unable to comply with
very reasonable requests, such as when it is time to switch the
computer off and join us all for tea. He can get very cross
about nothing and it can take a long time to calm him down.
But when he now says 'Mum' or 'Dad' and smiles at us with
such open love in his eyes, my own love for him is confirmed
and nourished with tremendous joy.*

Evie, adoptive parent

As an adoptive parent you may find that you need help to
understand your child's history of attachment – make sure you ask
lots of questions about this when you are linked with a child. You
need to be prepared for what might lie ahead, and you have to be
confident that you can manage this, with support if necessary. You
need to ensure that any help you or your child might need is outlined
in the Adoption Support Plan. A child with attachment difficulties
needs parents who are able to tolerate challenging behaviour and
who will work hard to understand it and not react to it. It can be
very difficult to keep your cool and work *therapeutically* with a child
who is behaving irrationally, but this is what you need to do; the key
to changing a child's behaviour is to manage *your* behaviour. Often
children with attachment difficulties do not respond to verbal ways
of communicating in the way you might expect. You need to relate

to the child at their emotional age, which might be quite a bit younger than their chronological age. You might need to find ways of communicating, other than verbal ones, such as through plenty of physical care for young children. Sensory care, such as massages and aromatherapy, can be helpful for you as well as for the child! It is important to give the child stimulating experiences and to build on things the child is good at in order to develop their resilience, self-esteem and confidence.

Much of this chapter has focused on the issues that can sometimes arise for children who have had difficult early years. But it is also important to appreciate the creativity, love and energy that children can bring to family life.

Reflection of my life

I am looking in the mirror and I am seeing my reflection,
I don't know why but it's ruining my perfection.
But what my reflection doesn't know, o! o!
And what my friends don't know, o! o!
Can't hurt them.
But if you really want to know then here you go.

I want to sing, I want to dance,
I want to touch the sky with my own two hands!
If I sing to the stars they could set me free and let me be who
I want to be.

So there you go.
You've heard what I want to be and you've heard what I want to do with my life today, and all through eternity.

Harry, aged nine

8

Adoption support

It's not easy being a parent. Whether you are caring for a newborn, vulnerable baby, or a teenager who disagrees with everything you say, there are challenges every day. All parents need support. Most parents have natural sources of support; grandparents and extended family members who can offer reassurance and help with the new baby, or friends with whom they can talk through the challenges posed by teenagers.

Parents sometimes need to turn to others for professional help and reassurance; to talk to the public health nurse (the health visitor) about feeding difficulties, for example, or to seek reassurance that the child is developing appropriately, or to see the family doctor about worries in relation to health matters. In relation to older children, parents might need to talk to teachers and this can sometimes trigger the involvement of other professional help if need be, such as an educational psychologist, a speech therapist or a social worker.

It's really important for people thinking of adoption to look at the support networks that you have got around you. We are from England and haven't got family up here so we haven't got people we can immediately fall back on. I think it's important for the adoptive parents to be able to get away and have a night out, let off a bit of steam and not lose sight of who they are as well as what they are trying to do. You have to be strong, but you need help and time for you.

Dave, adoptive parent

Parents of adopted children sometimes need more help and support than other parents, because of the complicated life experiences their children may have had and the traumatic times they might have endured prior to adoption. The amount of help and support adoptive families need varies. Some choose to manage things on their own, using the informal support that they have through their natural networks but others look for more formal support.

You need to build a "village of support" around you to help you cope. Professionals, neighbours, family, clubs, schools, the lot!

Lyndsay, adoptive parent

Given the sometimes challenging nature of adoption, legislation now requires that when placing a child for adoption, the adoption agency should draw up an Adoption Support Plan in consultation with the adoptive parents. Whilst some families do not feel the need for this, and choose to get on with their new lives with minimum intervention from adoption agencies, many welcome ongoing support. The Adoption Support Plan looks at the ongoing support that may be needed. Even if you decide you do not wish to have an Adoption Support Plan, you can request one at a later date if things change.

Adoption Support Plan

When your child first moves in with you, the adoption will not have been finalised. Even if the child is subject to a POA, you will have to wait for some weeks after submitting your adoption application to the court before the Adoption Order is granted. During this time the child cannot be removed from your care. You will receive visits from two social workers: the social worker for the child and the social worker from the adoption agency through which you were approved. The child's social worker has to ensure the needs of the child are being met, and the agency social worker visits to support you. The roles overlap. You should know your agency social worker well, particularly if they undertook your assessment and were there when you went to the adoption panel and were linked and matched with the child.

The first days and weeks of an adoption placement are a steep learning curve; you and the child need to begin to get to know each other and to start to form a relationship. During the introductory process you should have been given lots of information about the child and their routines, but the reality of being responsible for their care 24/7 can take some getting used to. Some adoptive families ease into the role without major difficulties, but for others it can take some time. If there is anything you want to talk about during this time, your first point of contact will normally be your social worker, but the child's social worker and the foster carers who cared for the child before they came to you can also help.

The Adoption Support Plan can cover the following:

- Whether adoption allowances will be paid and the amount of these.
- Whether any other payments will be made, for example, foster carers who adopt children in their care can sometimes continue to receive foster care fees for a time.
- Whether any particular support or therapies are needed for the child, such as speech therapy, play therapy or psychotherapy, and, if there is a cost, how this will be met.

- Whether you as adoptive parents might need any ongoing training and particular support, and how this will be provided.
- How any contact arrangements with the birth family or the child's previous foster carers will be managed.

The children did receive birthday cards from their birth mother, via the social worker, but these tailed off. Their father is dead. I made a point of sending photographs of the children to her every year, along with any news concerning them. I hope that was helpful for her. She eventually asked not to be sent any more information. My eldest daughter has now traced some of her birth family through Facebook. This can be an issue that some young people will need support with.

Jane, adoptive parent

The Adoption Support Plan should be reviewed periodically and altered as your needs for support change.

Some adoptive families have little contact with their agency after a while; it can tail off naturally as the child settles. Some families get the support they need from their own networks of friends and relatives.

It used to be the case that once a child was placed for adoption, contact between the adoption agency and the adoptive family would cease after a relatively short time and the family would be left to "get on with it!" It is now acknowledged that some children placed for adoption will need a great deal of support, sometimes for a long time. The local authority and the adoption agency, if different, both want the adoption to be a success and should do all they can to support you in the care of the child.

If you live in the local authority which previously had the care of the child, then that local authority will be responsible for providing adoption support until the child reaches the age of 18. If the child comes from a different local authority, then that local authority is responsible for adoption support for the first three years after the Adoption Order has been granted. After that, the local authority where you live becomes responsible. Both local authorities should make sure that the handover of support goes smoothly.

Financial and material support

The local authority has the power to pay adoptive parents an adoption allowance under certain circumstances. There is wide discretion in relation to this. Each local authority has its own adoption allowance scheme and these vary around the country. Allowances can be paid to cover one-off costs, such as legal fees and equipment, including a bed, bedding, buggy, etc. They can also be paid regularly on a time-limited basis, or over a longer period, for example to enable an adoptive parent to take some time off work or reduce their working hours if the child has particular needs. Examples of circumstances when adoption allowances are paid include:

- When it is difficult to find an adoptive family for the child because of their age, ethnicity or other circumstances.
- When the child needs to be placed with one or more siblings.
- When the child has particular care needs, which may relate to disability or past trauma.

If the child meets the criteria for an allowance, this will be recorded in the minute of the adoption panel that recommended that the child should be placed for adoption. So when you are linked to a child you will be told if an allowance might be payable. If you decide you would like to apply for an allowance you might have to provide details of your income and your outgoings. When considering the payment of an ongoing allowance, most local authorities take into account the financial circumstances of the adoptive parents. Help with legal costs and equipment is normally given regardless of the income of the adoptive parents.

The purpose of the adoption allowance is to help cover additional costs associated with caring for a child who has particular needs. All children require time and effort to look after them and have an impact on household finances, so an adoption allowance is not paid in the majority of cases. Parenthood is a lifestyle choice and the cost is part and parcel of that. But some children in need of adoption will be particularly costly to care for. If they have a disability they may be heavy on clothes or washing; there may be a need for a special vehicle. If a child has had a particularly traumatic history they may need therapeutic help and there may be additional costs associated with transport. Some children need full-time care and attention, so an adoptive parent may not be able to return to work. A sibling group can be demanding to care for, and again, an adoptive parent may not be able to work, at least for some time.

If the child is not eligible for an adoption allowance at the time of placement, an allowance can be paid in the future if circumstances change. It may become evident after placement, for example, that a child has experienced more past trauma than had been known previously and requires particular help or attention. In this case you should raise the matter with your adoption agency social worker or the child's social worker and they will advise you how to apply.

The level of allowance is determined by the local authority with responsibility for the child. It is usually of a similar level to a fostering allowance, but the amount varies from one local authority to another. You should be given a copy of the local authority's adoption allowance scheme if you ask for it.

If you are adopting a child from another part of the UK, the rules about adoption allowances will be different. Your adoption agency will need to clarify the position for you.

As mentioned previously, some prospective adoptive parents will initially have their child placed with them on a fostering basis, while the adoption is concluded. Most local authorities will pay a fostering allowance during this period, even if the child is not eligible for an adoption allowance. The reason for this is that while the child remains looked after by the local authority, you are acting as foster carers and should be given help with the cost of caring for the child. You may be asked to attend Children's Hearings and looked after reviews, so it is reasonable that you receive the same financial support as foster carers. Most foster carers receive a fee for caring for children. This is on top of the fostering allowance. It is unlikely that you will receive a fee, even while acting as a foster carer, because the intention is that you will become the child's parent, and you should not receive a reward payment for being a parent to that child. The exception to this is when foster carers have the care of a child and later decide that they wish to adopt the child. In this case, a fee can sometimes be paid for a time to help the foster carers to adjust financially.

If there are particular barriers to the adoption of children the local authority might help to overcome these, for example, by helping with the cost of building an extension to enable you to adopt a sibling group.

Adoption allowances are normally reviewed once a year. This is usually a paper exercise to see if your financial circumstances have changed and therefore if you are still eligible, and to check that the child still meets the criteria.

Financial help from the state

Once the adoption is finalised you are eligible for the same help from the state as you would be if the child was your birth child. This includes state benefits, tax credits, child benefit and so on. Any adoption allowance you receive should be disregarded in relation to such benefits. If the child has a disability or special needs, you might be entitled to Disability Living Allowance (this is in the process of being replaced by a new system of Personal Independence Payments). This contains mobility and care components. Eligibility is determined by an application process followed by a medical assessment.

Other help with care

If your child has particular needs or a disability you might be eligible for additional help from the local authority where you live. The local authority should treat you the same as it would treat a birth parent, and make provisions accordingly. This might include additional support for your child in the classroom, help with care costs or help around the home. You may be eligible for direct payments from the local authority to enable you to buy such services yourself or pay for personal assistants who you can employ. New legislation means that local authorities can arrange for help to be provided through arrangements called Self-Directed Support. This empowers people in need, and those caring for them, to receive a mixture of support that is tailor-made to meet their needs, including services provided direct by the local authority, by care agencies or by employed personal assistants.

Personal and emotional support

Adoptive parents vary in terms of the level of support they want from professionals, but you should feel able to ask for this when you need it. Some adoptive parents also find it useful to have less formal support from people who know about adoption. Some adoption agencies have "buddying" schemes, where new adoptive parents are matched with experienced adopters who can provide a sounding board and talk over issues and concerns. Some local authorities and voluntary adoption agencies provide support groups which you can attend to talk over issues. Sometimes social workers are present at these and sometimes they are self-help groups. Both can be very helpful sources of support. It can be very useful to attend these groups even if you do not feel you have any "problems" with your adoption. It is good to be open to learning and to develop deeper understanding of your child and your role as a parent.

Some support groups are set up specifically for adoptive parents who are experiencing particular challenges.

We have a group of adoptive parents who meet up for a coffee and chat and I asked them all what they would say to people thinking of adoption. The number one response was that you need to be strong as a couple and very united (or resilient if you are on your own); the children sometimes try to play one off against the other to manipulate you. The close second was that you need a great sense of humour, you need the ability to laugh at yourself and see humour where not everyone around you will. Everyone agreed that we are all parenting a lot longer than families with birth children; our children are emotionally behind by a number of years and their immaturity means that when most other parents can back off and relax a bit we will still be "full on" parents.

We all agreed that the life we had with our kids as youngsters was not as we had imagined it would be, like a sugar-coated image, but that we had enjoyed family life. It may not have been the same lifestyle our friends experienced with birth children, and not what we started out thinking it would be like. But our family was ours, of our making, and while that may be unusual in a birth family world, our families are not unique in an adoption world.

We all learned and agreed that high expectations are both harmful and put too much pressure on everyone. We had all accepted that the number one thing we wanted for our children is that they are happy. The expectations of adoptive parents in terms of family life have to be flexible; what may be very important to one family may be of little importance to another.

The one thing we all felt we should have done was ask for help more. At first, when our children were placed, we wanted everyone from the past out of their lives. That is not being negative, it's simply parents bonding with their child and wanting to get down to living together and claiming their child for their own. However, we all felt that we had spent too much time thinking we had to be super parents; we had felt we could not get it wrong after all the hoops we had jumped through to be allowed to adopt. How could we possibly go back and say that we were struggling? We had thought we might be judged and feel like a failure. Through experience we have learned that it is not a mark of failure to ask for help, but necessary to ensure we get the right help for our children and ourselves. Our children experience all the same problems as birth children growing up, but with a lot of extra pressures on top. We all felt we should have gone back for more training and support a lot earlier than we did, to help us understand our children better, and help us respond to our children's issues with more empathy.

Would we would do it all again? We asked each other to think what our lives would be like now without our children! No one could imagine living that life, probably because we are all parents and love our children no matter what.

Sarah, adoptive parent and support group co-ordinator

In addition to support groups, adoption agencies also provide ongoing training opportunities where speakers might talk and discuss common issues such as attachment, life story work, contact issues, how to manage challenging behaviour and so on. The programmes available will vary from one adoption agency to another. It is a good idea to check out what is available when you are thinking of applying to adopt, as this might affect your decision about which agency you apply to.

There are a number of agencies that provide specialist adoption support. Details of these can be found in Chapter 9.

Support for children and young people who have been adopted

Some children and young people need help to understand why they were adopted, and some wish to find out about their birth families or trace them when they are old enough to do so. In Scotland young people can do this at the age of 16. Some agencies provide counselling and support to children and young people in relation to this.

There was a time in my life when, on what should have been an amazing holiday in Australia, sailing around the Great Barrier Reef on a beautiful yacht with friends, at the age of 12, the questions started to rush around my brain – all the whys, the whens and the hows. I was bombarded with them. I felt heart-heavy, heartbroken, heartsick to think that this wasn't my "real" family. These emotions of rage, sadness and confusion led to me taking it out on my (adoptive) mum. The black beast of hate in my breast filled me with a resentment and loathing for my mother. I felt like Jekyll and Hyde, two different people, two split emotions fighting within me. I know I loved my (adoptive) mum, but still there was a nagging feeling of guilt that my love should only lie with my birth mum. Grief, pain and melancholy overcame me – was my life a living lie?

Assaulted by the barrage of questions, I had to have answers. I could not bring myself to ask my mum. She had told me why I was adopted from since I can remember. I've always known, but I wanted a thorough and deeper understanding and although she had provided me with all the essentials I needed, she could not provide me with this and I didn't want her to. I felt that it had come to the point where I was no longer comfortable asking her questions about my "other" mother and about why she had done what she had.

Fortunately for me, when we came back home, my mum saw how troubled and lost I was feeling at this time. She immediately looked for help and found it by getting in touch with the Scottish Adoption Services. That's when I met Kate. I felt that I could say things and in a way completely confide in Kate, things that I couldn't express to my mum without the fear of hurting her feelings. Through talking with Kate and asking questions, slowly, over time, I began to feel happier and gained a greater understanding about my adoption. That allowed me to feel at peace and be happy within myself. In addition to this process I met four other girls who had been adopted. I had never met other adopted people before apart from my brother! This inspiring and special experience showed me that there were others out there who had been in my shoes; I found that these girls I befriended each had a completely different adoption story and in some cases, worse than mine.

With the help of the Scottish Adoption Services I was glowing inside to know that I have such a caring and loving family. At this time I have resolved my questions and fears and looked to the future with an optimistic heart.

Emily, adopted young person

Sometimes children may present issues that will not have been foreseen. It is not uncommon for a child to disclose that they have been physically or sexually abused once they achieve the security of an adoptive placement. There may have been little or no indication of this beforehand. You will need to seek help in dealing with this.

Sometimes, if you already have birth children or other adopted children, relationships between them and the new child may not work out as you had hoped. There may be disputes about the amount of attention you are able to give them as parents, feelings of jealousy, tensions about space and belongings. Existing children can find the arrival of a new child difficult and the problems can become long term. It is sometimes easier if there is a decent age gap or if the profile of the children is quite different. The new family dynamics can feel overwhelming and it is important that you talk about these with your partner if you have one, with your informal support network and with professionals who are supporting you. Sometimes if your existing children are older you can talk to them too and help them to understand how the new child might be feeling and why he or she is behaving in the way they are.

Dealing with challenges

Adoptions don't always work out. There is little hard information about the rate of adoption breakdowns in Scotland. One local authority recently revealed that out of the last 70 adoptions they had made, only two had broken down. One voluntary adoption agency also said that about two per cent of their adoption placements have broken down in recent years. But what do we mean by breakdown, and what do we mean by success?

If an adoption placement comes to an end when a child is aged 15 and has been in placement for 10 years, is this a breakdown? And who is to say what would have become of the child if they had not been adopted? They might have had a series of foster and residential placements and a less positive outcome. In the 10 years they spent with the adoptive parents they could have had the best experience of being cared for that could be achieved for them. Eleanor, an adoptive parent, experienced an adoption breakdown after 12 years. She did all that she could to retain the care of her daughter, but in the end the young person, then aged 16, was determined that she wanted to live elsewhere. Despite this, Eleanor did not regret the adoption, and still felt her life had been enriched by what had obviously been a very difficult experience. Not all adoptive parents who experience these issues can be so philosophical. There can be a lot of pain, guilt and anger when things go wrong. Sometimes children can reject the values of their adoptive parents and this can be very hurtful and difficult to manage.

The teenage years are difficult for many parents, both of adopted children and birth children, and this can be a time when family relationships become stressful and break down in some families. Fortunately, adoption breakdowns are not common, and as we understand the nature of children's difficulties more and more, and get better at preparing and supporting adoptive families, it is to be hoped that they will become less frequent still.

Footnote

There are hundreds of children in need of adoptive families in
Scotland. All of them are different and some of them will be
challenging to care for because of the difficult start they had in life.
They need families who are prepared to take time to understand
their needs, and who can be patient and consistent; families with the
time, energy and commitment to learn special parenting skills. It is
hard work to be a good parent, and it can be harder still if your child
is adopted. But none of the adoptive parents who contributed to this
book say they regret their decision to adopt. They have found
adoption to be fulfilling and to have enriched their lives. Even those
who have been really tested say their lives would have been empty
without their children.

If you decide to adopt, your life will change forever. You will face
challenges along the way. The process of adoption can be long. You
can feel judged during the assessment and the legal stage can feel
daunting. But hundreds of families get through this process every
year, and it is heartwarming to hear stories of families being formed
and looking to the future with hope and confidence.

---

*Adoption is the best thing I have done. I just absolutely love
my children. To me they are my flesh and blood. I think it's
really hard for social workers to convey the reality to
prospective adopters. I can only say that it has been the most
emotionally challenging job I ever did in my life and will ever
do in my life, but even though some days are hard, being a
parent is fantastic. I just want to burst with pleasure every
time I think they are my children.*

Shona, adoptive parent

9

Information and help

This chapter gives details of how to contact adoption agencies and provides brief information about some agencies that can offer help and support to people affected by adoption.

Local authority adoption agencies

The details for the 32 Scottish local authority adoption agencies are given below. Details of the services they provide can be found on their websites or by making contact with them.

Aberdeen City Council
Adoption and Fostering Service
77-79 King Street
Aberdeen
AB24 5AB
Tel: 01224 793830
Email: adoptfost@aberdeencity.gov.uk
www.aberdeencity.gov.uk

Aberdeenshire Council
Social Work Department
Carlton House
Arduthie Road
Stonehaven
AB39 2DL
Tel: 01467 625555
Email: adoption@aberdeenshire.gov.uk
www.aberdeenshire.gov.uk

Angus Council
Family Placement Team
Academy Lane
Arbroath
DD11 1EJ
Tel: 01241 435078
Email: fosteringandadoption@angus.gov.uk
www.angus.gov.uk

Argyll and Bute Council
Community Services
Children and Families
Kilmory
Lochgilphead
PA31 8RT
Tel: 01546 605517
Email: fpduty@argyll-bute.gov.uk
www.argyll-bute.gov.uk

Clackmannanshire Council
Child Care Services
Lime Tree House
Castle Street
Alloa
FK10 1EX
Tel: 01259 225000
Email: childcare@clacks.gov.uk
www.clacksweb.org.uk

Comhairle Nan Eilean Siar (Western Isles Council)
Social Work Department
Council Offices
Rathad Shanndabhaig (Sandwick Road)
Steornabhagh (Stornoway)
Isle of Lewis
HS1 2BW
Tel: 0845 600 7090
Email: enquiries@cne-siar.gov.uk
www.cne-siar.gov.uk

Dumfries & Galloway Council
Fostering and Adoption Team
122-124 Irish Street
Dumfries
DG1 2AW
Tel: 01387 273600
Email: sandra.ritchie@dumgal.gov.uk
www.dumgal.gov.uk

Dundee City Council
Dudhope Castle
Barrack Road
Dundee
DD3 6HF
Tel: 01382 436060
www.dundeecity.gov.uk

East Ayrshire Council
Fostering and Adoption Team
The Johnnie Walker Bond
15 Strand Street
Kilmarnock
East Ayrshire
KA1 1HU
Tel: 0800 434 6633
Email: fosteringandadoption@east-ayrshire.gov.uk
www.east-ayrshire.gov.uk

East Dunbartonshire Council
Social Work
Adoption and Fostering
Southbank House
Strathkelvin Place
Kirkintilloch
G66 1XQ
Tel: 0141 777 3003
Email: familybasedcare@eastdunbarton.gov.uk
www.eastdunbarton.gov.uk

East Lothian Council
The Family Placement Team
Randall House
Macmerry Business Park
Macmerry
EH33 1RW
Tel: 01620 827643
Email: familyplacement@eastlothian.gov.uk
www.eastlothian.gov.uk

East Renfrewshire Council
Fostering and Adoption
Lygates House
224 Ayr Road
Newton Mearns
East Renfrewshire
G77 6FR
Tel: 0141 577 3367
www.eastrenfrewshire.gov.uk

City of Edinburgh Council
Family Based Care Recruitment Team
Springwell House
1 Gorgie Road
Edinburgh
EH11 2LA

Tel: 0800 174 833
Email: foster.children@edinburgh.gov.uk
www.edinburgh.gov.uk

Falkirk Council
Social Work Services
Adoption and Fostering Team
Grangemouth Social Work Office
Oxgang Road
Grangemouth
FK3 9EF
Tel: 01324 504343
Email: fosteringandadoptionteam@falkirk.gov.uk
www.falkirk.gov.uk

Fife Council
Family Placement Team
New City House
1 Edgar Street
Dunfermline
KY12 7EP
Tel: 0345 155 5555
www.fifedirect.org.uk

Glasgow City Council
Families for Children
136 Stanley Street
Glasgow
G41 1JH
Tel: 0845 270 0609
Email: families.children@sw.glasgow.gov.uk
www.glasgow.gov.uk

Highland Council
Family Resource Centre
Limetree Avenue
Inverness

IV3 5RH
Tel: 01463 703431
Email: fostering@highland.gov.uk
www.highland.gov.uk

Inverclyde Council
Social Work
Children and Families Section
Ravenscraig Hospital
Inverkip Road
Greenock
PA16 9HA
Tel: 01475 714039
www.inverclyde.gov.uk

Midlothian Council
Family Placement Team
Adoption and Fostering
Lawfield Primary School
26 Lawfield Road
Mayfield
Dalkeith
EH22 5BB
Tel: 0131 270 5678
Email: family.placement@midlothian.gov.uk
www.midlothian.gov.uk

Moray Council
Fostering and Adoption Team
6 Moss Street
Elgin
Moray
IV30 1LU
Tel: 01343 563568
Email: foster.adopt@moray.gov.uk
www.moray.gov.uk

North Ayrshire Council
The Family Placement Team
Social Services
47 West Road
Irvine
Ayrshire
KA12 8RE
Tel: 01294 311505
Email: adfos@north-ayrshire.gov.uk
www.north-ayrshire.gov.uk

North Lanarkshire Council
Fostering and Adoption Team
Social Work Department
Children's Carers' Centre
7 Mitchell Street
Airdrie
ML6 0EB
Tel: 0800 073 1566
Email: northrecservices@northlan.gov.uk
www.northlan.gov.uk

Orkney Islands Council
Children and Families Team
Council Offices
School Place
Kirkwell
KW15 1NY
Tel: 01856 873535
Email: social.services@orkney.gov.uk
www.orkney.gov.uk

Perth & Kinross Council
Permanence Team
Colonsay Resource Centre
Perth
PH1 3TU

Tel: 01738 783450
Email: ecsfosteringandadoption@pkc.gov.uk
www.pkc.gov.uk

Renfrewshire Council

Renfrewshire Fostering and Adoption Services
Paisley Locality Office
Abbey House
8 Seedhill Road
Paisley
PA1 1JT
Tel: 0300 300 1199
Email: childrenandfamilies.sw@renfrewshire.gov.uk
www.renfrewshire.gov.uk

Scottish Borders Council

Adoption, Fostering and Family Placement Team
Paton Street
Galashiels
TD1 3DL
Tel: 01896 662799
www.scotborders.gov.uk

Shetland Islands Council

Family Placement Team
Hayfield House
Hayfield Lane
Lerwick
Shetland
ZE1 0QD
Tel: 01595 744400
Email: fosteringandadoptionteam@shetland.gov.uk
www.shetland.gov.uk

South Ayrshire Council

Family Placement and Adoption Team
Whitletts Area Centre

181 Whitletts Road
Ayr
KA8 0JQ
Tel: 01292 267675
Email: fostering@south-ayrshire.gov.uk
www.south-ayrshire.gov.uk

South Lanarkshire Council
Social Work Department
Adoption and Fostering
4th Floor
Brandongate
1 Leachlee Road
Hamilton
ML3 0XB
Tel: 01698 454895
Email: familyplacement@southlanarkshire.gov.uk
www.southlanarkshire.gov.uk

Stirling Council
Adoption
Municipal Buildings
8-10 Corn Exchange Road
Stirling
FK8 2HU
Tel: 01786 471177
Email: adoption-fostering@stirling.gov.uk
www.stirling.gov.uk

West Dunbartonshire Council
The Adoption and Fostering Team
West Dunbartonshire
CHCP Childcare Section
1st Floor
Bridge Street
Dumbarton
G82 1NT

Tel: 01389 772165/772166
Email: fostering@west-dunbarton.gov.uk
www.west-dunbarton.gov.uk

Western Isles Council
See Comhairle nan eilean siar

West Lothian Council
The Family Placement Team
189a West Main Street
Broxburn
West Lothian
EH52 5LH
Tel: 01506 775677
www.westlothian.gov.uk

Voluntary adoption agencies that recruit adoptive families

There are four voluntary adoption agencies that recruit adoptive parents in Scotland.

Barnardo's Scotland Adoption Placement Service
One of the largest children's charities in the UK, Barnardo's has been an approved adoption agency since 1947, and has more than 100 years' experience of finding families for children. The adoption service is part of the wider Barnardo's Scotland organisation, which works with more than 10,000 children, young people and their families across Scotland through the provision of specialist services. The Adoption Placement Team was launched in November 2011. It provides placements for children from a variety of backgrounds including sibling groups, under-5s who may have additional support needs, single children aged five and over and children from any ethnic, cultural or religious background.

The Adoption Placement Team provides assessment and preparation training to prospective adopters and, once approved, supports them in the placement of children and their aftercare. The service places children from local authorities all over Scotland.

Barnardo's Scotland Adoption Placement Service
Suite 5/3, Skypark SP5
45 Finnieston Street
Glasgow
G3 8JU
Tel 0141 222 4700
Email: adoptscot@barnardos.org.uk
www.barnardos.org.uk

Scottish Adoption

This national organisation was established in 1923 with the aim of delivering high quality placement and adoption services. Most services are currently delivered across Edinburgh and Lothians, along with a range of inter-agency work with organisations in other parts of Scotland. All staff are professionally qualified with specific experience in adoption. The agency is continually researching and developing new approaches to meet the changing needs of service users, and "looks after people every step of the way, with a commitment to support all their adopted children and families for however long and whenever this is needed."

Scottish Adoption
161 Constitution Street
Leith
Edinburgh
EH6 7AD
Tel: 0131 553 5060
Email: info@scottishadoption.org
www.scottishadoption.org

St Andrew's Children's Society

The Society was founded by the Roman Catholic Church in Scotland in 1922 to place young, relinquished babies for adoption. In response to changing social trends in the 1970s, it then began finding families for children in public care who needed permanence. St Andrew's Children's Society no longer has any formal links with the Catholic Church but continues to provide an adoption service to the Catholic community as well as to the wider public. It operates within a 60-mile radius of Edinburgh, with a further office about to open in the North of Scotland.

The Society recruits, trains, and approves adoptive parents and foster carers, and supports and advises adopters and children for as long as necessary. It also helps adopted children keep in touch with their birth family, when appropriate, through the exchange of information and sometimes by direct contact, and offers counselling and support to adopted adults who want to understand the circumstances of their adoption, as well as to all birth family members affected by adoption.

St Andrew's Children's Society
7 John's Place
Leith
Edinburgh
EH6 7EL
Tel: 0131 454 3370
Email: info@standrews-children.org.uk
www.standrews-children.org.uk

St Margaret's Children and Family Care Society

The Society was founded in 1955 as an initiative by the Catholic Church in Scotland to find adoptive parents for babies. St Margaret's now recruits adoptive parents and foster carers, of all faiths and none, for children in public care, and offers counselling to mothers thinking of relinquishing their child for adoption. The Society provides support to adoptive families, both immediately after adoption and on a longer-term basis. It offers a service for birth parents who are keeping in letterbox contact with adopted children. It has archive material relating to many children adopted as babies, and provides support to adults accessing this. St Margaret's works closely with local authorities and other agencies, and takes part in research and development activities relating to adoption. Most work centres around the Glasgow area.

St Margaret's Children and Family Care Society
274 Bath Street
Glasgow
G2 4JR
Tel: 0141 332 8371
Email: info@stmargaretsadoption.org.uk
www.stmargaretsadoption.org.uk

Other sources of information and support

Adoption UK
Adoption UK is a UK-wide charity, founded by adoptive parents, that works with and on behalf of adoptive parents, prospective adopters and long-term foster carers, offering information, support and a vibrant adoption community before, during and after adoption. Adoption UK runs a family-finding service called Children Who Wait, bringing together children and parents. This is available to Adoption UK members in magazine and online form, and profiles in the region of 200 children waiting for adoption each month.

Adoption UK in Scotland helps parents understand the needs of their adopted children, and works to help adoptive families access support, information and training. From the Edinburgh office, Adoption UK provides: a dedicated Scottish helpline that is open to all; a specialist Family Support Service; a range of innovative support group activities; facilitated family events that enable adoptive families to meet up and develop ongoing friendships; and conferences and training for both parents and professionals.

Adoption UK
172 Leith Walk
Edinburgh
EH6 5EA

Tel: 0131 5555 350
Email: scotland@adoptionuk.org.uk
www.adoptionuk.org

Barnardo's Scotland Adoption Support Service (SASS)

SASS is a post adoption service providing a range of services to anyone whose life is affected by adoption. It is based in Glasgow and offers services to people living in 15 local authorities across Scotland. It recognises the lifelong implications of adoption for all involved.

It recognises that adoptive parents and children can face many challenges, including difficult background information about and/or contact with birth family members. Social networking may also present issues. SASS offers a range of support services to children and families. These include working with the family as a whole, working individually with children, providing individual sessions for parents, and offering support groups and workshops. It can help children gain a more coherent understanding of their past. It can also explore with parents more effective methods of parenting and provide mediation and support in contact with the birth family. It can also offer therapeutic input through two psychotherapists employed by Barnardo's.

Barnardo's Scotland Adoption Support Service
Suite 5/3
Skypark SP5
45 Finnieston Street
Glasgow
G3 8JU
Tel: 0141 222 4700
Email: adoptscot@barnardos.org.uk
www.barnardos.org.uk

Birthlink

Birthlink provides an After Adoption Information Line for anyone who has been affected by adoption. The service is used by adopted adults, birth parents of people adopted as children and their family

members, adoptive family members and social workers. Birthlink's
Care Connect service helps adults who were formerly in public care
to access information from records. The Adoption Contact register
puts adopted people and their birth parents or relatives in touch with
each other when both parties want this to happen.

Birthlink
21 Castle Street
Edinburgh
EH2 3DN
Tel: 0131 225 6441
Email: mail@birthlink.org.uk
www.birthlink.org.uk

British Association for Adoption and Fostering (BAAF)

BAAF has been supporting, advising and campaigning for better
outcomes for children in public care for over 30 years. They work
with everyone involved in adoption and fostering across the UK.
They undertake research, publish lots of books about adoption and
promote and develop adoption and fostering services. There is an
office in Edinburgh, from which services are provided to the whole of
Scotland. They provide support, advice and training to adoptive
families and to professionals.

BAAF Scotland
113 Rose Street
Edinburgh
EH2 3DT
Tel: 0131 226 9270
Email: scotland@baaf.org.uk
www.baaf.org.uk/scotland

The Care Inspectorate

This is the independent scrutiny and improvement body for care
services in Scotland. Its aim is to ensure that people receive high
quality care and that services protect their rights. The Care
Inspectorate registers and inspects all adoption and fostering

agencies in Scotland. Inspection reports are published on their website. The Care Inspectorate can look into complaints about services.

The Care Inspectorate
Compass House
11 Riverside Drive
Dundee
DD1 4NY
Tel: 0845 600 9527
Email: enquiries@careinspectorate.com
www.scswis.com

The Fostering Network

The Fostering Network is a leading charity for foster care. As the "voice of foster care" the Fostering Network influences policy and campaigns for improvements throughout the UK. It provides training, resources, information and advice about all aspects of fostering – from how to become a foster carer to issues around pay, insurance, child care law and allegations – through a helpline service called Fosterline Scotland.

The Fostering Network
Ingram House
2nd Floor
227 Ingram Street
Glasgow
G1 1DA
Tel: 0141 204 1400
Email: scotland@fostering.net
www.fostering.net

New Family Social

A national charity that provides support and information for prospective, and existing, lesbian, gay, bisexual and transgender (LGBT) adopters and foster carers. It has about 600 members. It aims to widen the pool of new parents for children waiting for adoption.

It connects LGBT adopters with others in similar situations. It has a support network in Scotland.

New Family Social
PO Box 66244
London
E9 9BD
Tel: 0843 289 9457
www.newfamilysocial.org.uk

The Scottish Government

The Scottish Government website has links to legislation, regulations and guidance, including that related to adoption and fostering. The website can be used to search for particular information, including intercountry adoption.

www.scotland.gov.uk

10

Useful reading

Except where marked, these publications are available from BAAF. Visit www.baaf.org.uk or contact BAAF Publications on 020 7421 2604 for more details or to order.

Books about adoption

PERSONAL NARRATIVES

An Adoption Diary
MARIA JAMES
This is an inspirational real-life account of one couple's emotional journey to become a family, which gives a fascinating insight into adoption today. Spanning four years, the diary covers assessment, the months of waiting, and finally the match with a two-year-old boy.
BAAF 2006

Flying Solo
JULIA WISE
Julia Wise gave up a high-flying career and hectic London life to move to the country and adopt a child on her own. This heart-warming and humorous account will resonate loudly with single adopters everywhere.
BAAF 2007

In Black and White
NATHALIE SEYMOUR
This honest account follows Nathalie and Tom, a white couple living in 1970s Britain, who decided to establish a transracial adopted

family. Further, they wanted the children to remain connected with their birth family. An intriguing and absorbing story.

BAAF 2007

Adoption Undone

KAREN CARR

This is the true story of an adoption and an adoption breakdown, bravely told by the adoptive mother. From the final court hearing when Lucy returned to local authority care, Karen Carr looks back over a tale of loss and regret, but also courage, generosity and self-discovery.

BAAF 2007

Together in Time

RUTH AND ED ROYCE

From a dual perspective, each with their own anxieties and expectations, Ruth and Ed Royce record their decision to adopt, their son's deep-seated problems, and how their experience of music and art therapy helped them to come together as a family…and to adopt for a second time.

BAAF 2008

The Family Business

ROBERT MARSDEN

This is the story of the adoption of William, a little boy with cerebral palsy, by a middle-aged couple with three birth children. Narrated by the adoptive father, this positive, upbeat account describes adopting a child with a disability and the impact of adoption on the whole family.

BAAF 2008

Take Two

LAUREL ASHTON

This moving story follows Laurel and David through their discovery of their infertility, months of treatment, and eventual decision to adopt. Their adoption of Amber, a baby girl, and then of Emily, are narrated, as Laurel remembers the first months of family life.

BAAF 2008

The Colours in Me

PERLITA HARRIS (ed.)

In this unique collection of poetry, prose and artwork, over 80 adopted children and young people tell it like it is, revealing what it feels like and what it means to be adopted. With extraordinary clarity and candour they describe the huge changes that adoption brings and the impact of these changes on their identity, their relationships and their understanding of the meaning of "family".

BAAF 2008

I Wish I Had Been Born From You

Written by a mother, with contributions from her adopted daughter, this honest and heartfelt collection charts a moving and emotional adoption journey of getting to know one another and becoming a family.

BAAF 2009

Dale's Tale

HELEN JAYNE

The story of Helen, a foster carer, and her family, and what happened when a short-term foster placement – of Dale, a young boy – became longer than expected. When Helen decides she wants to adopt Dale, the agencies involved definitely have other ideas.

BAAF 2010

Holding on and Hanging in

JACKIE WHITE

This compelling journey tracks Wayne's journey, from first being fostered by Lorna at the age of nine, in a "therapeutic" foster placement, through nearly four years of family life. Wayne is traumatised by his early experiences, and helping him to heal and grow is a long and difficult process, but one which Lorna is determined to persevere in.

BAAF 2010

Frozen
MIKE BUTCHER

When husband and wife Mike and Lesley embark on a course of IVF treatment, they are full of hope for a successful outcome – a child they can call their own. But after a shocking reaction to the treatment, and an escalating series of setbacks and heartache, they are forced to put their dream on hold – until they look into adoption.

BAAF 2010

When Daisy met Tommy
JULES BELLE

This is the real-life story of how six-year-old Daisy and her parents adopted Tom. Honest and accessible, it charts the ups and downs of the adoption process, as experienced by a daughter already in the family.

BAAF 2010

Becoming Dads
PABLO FERNÁNDEZ

This is the story of Pablo and Mike and their journey to becoming adopters. Set against a contemporary backdrop of diverse perceptions as to whether gay men should adopt, Pablo's diarised narrative tracks this journey starting from their own initial doubts about being accepted and approved, through to their joy at becoming the proud dads of a young boy.

BAAF 2011

Is It True You Have Two Mums?
RUBY CLAY

Ruby and Gail believe they have the potential to adopt. Some social workers they encounter think that, as a lesbian couple, they are unfit to be parents; others recognise that their Asian dual-heritage family has much to offer. This honest account charts their journey to becoming parents to three adopted daughters and offers a glimpse of their family life over 18 extraordinary years.

BAAF 2011

As If I Was A Real Boy

GORDON AND JEANNIE MACKENZIE

This is the inspirational story of how Gordon, who was 10 and living in a psychiatric hospital with undiagnosed mental health issues, was adopted by Jeannie. In a moving account, mother and son look back at the way in which adoption changed their two lives for the better.

BAAF 2011

Finding our Familia

STEVAN WHITEHEAD

This is the true story of the adoption of two children from Guatemala. It also provides a moving and inspirational account of how a couple, in their search to build their family, find not only two children but also a group of people who will become their extended family – their *familia*.

BAAF 2012

Chosen

PERLITA HARIS (ed.)

This thought-provoking collection of first-hand accounts explores the lifelong impact of adoption. It brings together writing and poetry by over 50 UK adopted adults born between 1934 and 1984. Through a broad range of perspectives they capture the life-changing power of adoption and the different meanings it can take on at different stages in one's life.

BAAF 2012

From China with Love

EMILY BUCHANAN

A moving account of a couple's experiences as they go through the process of adopting a child from China.

Wiley 2006

ADOPTION: DIFFERENT ASPECTS

The Adopter's Handbook

AMY NEIL SALTER

This guide sets out clear, accurate information about adoption before, during and after the big event, to help adopters help themselves throughout the adoption process and beyond. Topics covered include education, health and adoption support (although some information may be England specific).

BAAF 2013 (fifth edition)

Attachment, Trauma and Resilience

KATE CAIRNS

Drawing on Kate's personal experiences with three birth children and 12 fostered children, this book describes family life with children who have experienced attachment difficulties, loss and trauma. Using knowledge and ideas drawn from attachment theory, the author suggests what can be done to promote recovery and develop resilience.

BAAF 2002

Related by adoption: A handbook for grandparents and other carers

HEDI ARGENT

This handbook aims to give grandparents and other relatives information about adoption today that directly affects them. It discusses how the wider family can support building a family through adoption and be involved in both the good and the bad times.

BAAF 2004

'Just a member of the family': Families and children who adopt

BRIDGET BETTS, VIDEO/DVD

This is the first film to look at adoption from a child's point of view, featuring a number of birth children who have had the experience of adopting a child into their family.

BAAF 2005

The Adoption Experience: Families who give children a second chance

ANN MORRIS

Actual adopters tell it like it is on every part of the adoption process from the exciting moment of first deciding to adopt to feelings about children seeking a reunion with their natural families or simply leaving home.

Jessica Kingsley Publishers for Adoption UK in association with the Daily Telegraph 1999

ADOPTION: PARENTING

The Parenting Matters series

This unique series provides expert knowledge about a range of children's health conditions, coupled with facts, figures and guidance presented in a straightforward and accessible style. Adopters and foster carers also describe what it is like to parent an affected child, "telling it like it is", sharing their parenting experiences and offering useful advice. This combination will help readers to gain knowledge, achieve understanding and to make informed decisions about whether they can care for a child with a health need or condition they may otherwise know little about or have no direct experience of. Titles in the series explore **Attention Deficit Hyperactivity Disorder**, **Autism Spectrum Disorder**, **Developmental Delay**, **Dyslexia**, **Emotional and Behavioural Difficulties**, **Mental Health Issues** and **Parental Substance Misuse**.

Talking about Adoption to your Adopted Child

MARJORIE MORRISON

A guide to the whys, whens, and hows of telling adopted children about their origins.

BAAF 2012 (fifth edition)

Adoption Conversations: What, when and how to tell

RENÉE WOLFS

This in-depth practical guide, written by an adoptive parent, explores the questions adopted children are likely to ask, with suggestions for helpful explanations and answers. Although the guide focuses primarily on children adopted from abroad, the advice given is applicable to any adopted child. A second book, *More Adoption Conversations* (2010), by the same author, looks specifically at adopted young people aged 13–18.

BAAF 2008

Looking After our Own: The stories of black and Asian adopters

EDITED BY HOPE MASSIAH

An inspiring collection looking at the experiences of nine black and Asian adoptive families and their children.

BAAF 2005

First Steps in Parenting the Child who Hurts: Tiddlers and toddlers (2nd edition)

CAROLINE ARCHER

This book offers practical, sensitive guidance from an adoptive parent through the areas of separation, loss and trauma in early childhood which will encourage confidence in other adoptive parents and foster carers and thereby enable enjoyment in parenting young children.

Jessica Kingsley Publishers for Adoption UK 1999

Next Steps in Parenting the Child who Hurts: Tykes and teens

CAROLINE ARCHER

Follows on from the *First Steps* book and shows how love can be expressed towards the older adopted child, despite persistent and often extreme tests of that love. Includes a review of specific sensitive situations that commonly arise and suggests some solutions.

Jessica Kingsley Publishers for Adoption UK 1999

Advice Notes

BAAF's popular leaflet series called Advice Notes contains essential information about key areas in adoption and fostering.

Adoption – some questions answered (2012)
Basic information about adoption. Explains the adoption process including the legal issues and the rights of birth parents.

Contact – if you are adopting a child (2009)
Explains what contact is and why it is important after adoption. Provides information on the purpose and practicalities of contact arrangements and the support available.

The preparation and assessment process (adoption) (2010)
Aimed at prospective adopters who have started the process with an agency. Explores preparation and assessment and what it involves.

Children's special needs – some questions answered (2010)
Information on the special needs that adopted and fostered children may have, for people considering adopting or fostering.

Stepchildren and adoption (Scotland) (2010)
Information for birth parents and step-parents on the advantages or not of adoption, and obtaining further advice. Editions also available for England and Wales.

Intercountry adoption – some questions answered (2011)
Information on adopting a child from overseas, including procedures, legislation, and where to obtain advice.

Children adopted from abroad – key health and developmental issues (2004)
Gives advice on the health and medical issues you may encounter if adopting a child from overseas.

Periodicals listing children who need new families

Be My Parent and Be My Parent online
A UK-wide monthly newspaper and website for adopters and
permanent foster carers who may or may not be approved. It
contains features on adoption and fostering and profiles of children
across the UK who need new permanent families. Subscription
details available from: 020 7421 2666.

Scottish Children Waiting
Scotland's Adoption Register produces a quarterly newsletter of
children awaiting placement for adoption in Scotland. This is
distributed to local authorities and voluntary adoption agencies and
is available to approved adopters. Further details available from:
0131 226 9279.

Adoption Today
Adoption Today is a monthly journal published by Adoption UK and
is available on subscription. It keeps members in touch with one
another, profiles children needing new permanent families, and gives
information on general developments in the field of adoption.
Further details available from: 01295 752240.

BAAF produces a large variety of other books about adoption,
including a wide selection of books for use with children. For more
details, visit www.baaf.org.uk or contact 020 7421 2604 for a
catalogue.

Glossary

This section explains some of the terms that have been used in this book and that you will come across if you go on to adopt a child.

Adoption agency
An organisation approved by the Care Inspectorate on behalf of the Scottish Government to provide adoption services. All Scottish local authorities act as adoption agencies. In addition there are four voluntary adoption agencies (VAAs) that recruit and approve adoptive parents and a small number of voluntary agencies that provide other services in relation to adoption.

Adoption allowance
An allowance that local authorities can pay to adoptive parents in relation to children who might not otherwise be adopted because they have additional needs or because the adoptive parents might otherwise experience financial difficulties.

Adoption Order
An order granted by a court that transfers to adoptive parents all the rights and responsibilities in relation to a child.

Adoption panel
A group of people with appropriate qualifications and experience who make recommendations to the adoption agency about whether a child should be adopted, whether adoptive applicants should be approved and whether a child should be matched with particular adoptive parents.

Adoption petition
An application made to a court to adopt a particular child.

Adoption Register
Scotland's Adoption Register is funded by the Scottish Government. It holds information about children waiting for adoption and about adoptive parents who have been approved by an adoption agency. The register tries to match the needs of children with the profiles of

families. N.B. Not all children or approved adoptive families are referred to the register. Adopters cannot self-refer to the register; all referrals must come via a social worker.

Adoption Services Plan
A strategic plan that has to be prepared by local authorities which sets down how they are going to meet the needs of anyone affected by adoption, including children, prospective adoptive parents and birth families whose children have been placed for adoption.

Adoption Support Plan
A plan that should be drawn up by local authorities in consultation with adoptive parents, setting down the arrangements for supporting the child and the adoptive family after the child has been placed for adoption. The placing local authority is responsible for implementing the plan for the first three years following adoption. Responsibility then transfers to the local authority where the adoptive family lives, if this is different.

Agency decision maker
A person appointed by an adoption agency who considers the recommendation of adoption panels and makes a decision about these on behalf of the agency.

Attachment disorder
A term that indicates that a child has not experienced sensitive care from his or her parents or carers and who consequently finds it difficult to trust and relate to others and who might not behave predictably.

Birth parent
The mother who gave birth to the child or the man who fathered the child. Sometimes also known as the natural parent, or biological parent, or "tummy mummy".

British Association of Adoption and Fostering (BAAF)
A voluntary agency that works across the UK to promote the needs of looked after children , particularly in relation to adoption and fostering (see Chapter 9).

Care Inspectorate

A Scottish Government agency that has responsibility for the registration and inspection of care services including those provided by adoption agencies. Inspection reports of all adoption agencies can be found on the website of the Care Inspectorate.

Children's Hearing

A meeting of children's panel members to consider the needs of individual children, whether they might be in need of care or supervision and how this should be provided.

Children's panel

Members of the public who are appointed through the Scottish Government to make decisions about the care of children, backed up by law.

Compulsory Supervision Order (CSO)

A legal order made by a Children's Hearing that places the child under the supervision of the local authority. Children can be subject to supervision while living with their birth parents or other relatives. The CSO can contain conditions that a child has to live in a certain place, such as with foster carers (commonly known as being in care). The CSO replaced the Supervision Requirement that was in place before the Children's Hearings (Scotland) Act 2011.

Contact

An arrangement whereby a birth parent or relative might have contact with, or information about, the child before or after he or she has been adopted. Indirect contact can be termed letterbox contact and involves birth parents or other significant figures being sent information and photographs about the child, usually once or twice a year.

Curator ad litem

A solicitor, social worker or someone with relevant qualifications who is appointed by the court to prepare a report which makes recommendations about whether adoption is in the best interests of the child. The curator undertakes this work after the child has been placed with the adoptive parents.

Disclosure Scotland
An agency set up by the Scottish Government that undertakes checks in relation to the criminal histories of those who work with or care for children, including prospective adoptive parents.

Disruption
The term used to describe an adoption placement that has broken down. A disruption meeting should be called after such a breakdown to look at the reasons for this, and to consider what should happen next and what can be learned from the experience.

Form E
A form designed by BAAF to assess the needs of children needing adoption or long-term care. A Child's Adoption and Permanence Report is being developed to replace the current format.

Form F
A form designed by BAAF and used by many adoption agencies to assess and profile adoptive applicants.

Home study
The process through which a social worker from an adoption agency assesses the applicants' potential to adopt and, together with the prospective adopters, considers the type of child they are best suited to care for.

Information Exchange Days
Events that profile children using written descriptions, accounts by their current carers, videos, and drawings and writings made by the children themselves. There may be an opportunity to meet the social worker and foster carer for the child. The events are open to approved adoptive parents to attend.

Kinship care
Arrangements where relatives or occasionally friends care for children. Sometimes such children are looked after through the Children's Hearing system, but often there is no legal order.

Legal advisor
A suitably qualified person who advises the adoption panel on legal matters concerning the child and prospective adopters.

Life story book

An account of the child's life designed to help him or her make sense of all that has happened in their past. Usually illustrated with photographs and notes and drawings.

Medical advisor

A doctor who advises the adoption panel on medical issues relating to the child or the adoptive applicants. Medical advisors are usually able to meet with prospective adoptive parents to give detailed information about the health needs of particular children.

Permanence Order

An order made by the sheriff court that transfers some of the parental responsibilities in relation to the child from the birth parent to the local authority. Some responsibilities might be given to foster carers or others as part of this arrangement.

Permanence Order with Authority to Adopt (POA)

An order that empowers the local authority to place the child with prospective adoptive parents, with the expectation that the child will be adopted by them.

Preparation group

A training course run by adoption agencies for prospective adoptive parents to help them understand what is involved in adopting a child and prepare them for the experience of adoption. Usually run in the evenings and sometimes at weekends.

Private fostering

An arrangement where someone who is not closely related to the child cares for them with the agreement of their parents. Parents and private foster carers must tell the local authority about this arrangement, and the local authority has to visit and undertake checks.

Reporting Officer

A solicitor or other suitably qualified person who is appointed by the court to report on the views and position of birth parents in relation to adoption. Often the same person as the curator.

Residence Order
An order granted by a court following a private application by someone who wishes to have responsibility for the care of a child. The order lasts till the child is 16 years old. The child is not looked after.

Safeguarder/Children's safeguarder
A solicitor, social worker or another suitably qualified person who is appointed by a Children's Hearing to provide an opinion about the plan for the child. Such an appointment is usually made when there are different views between those involved in considering the child's future.

Sibling
A brother or sister.